How to Get ON Reality TV

Matthew Robinson

Random House Reference
New York Toronto London Sydney Auckland

Please address inquiries about electronic licensing of any products for use on a network, in software, or on CD-ROM to the Subsidiary Rights Department, Random House Information Group, fax 212-572-6003.

This book is available for special discounts for bulk purchases for sales promotions or premiums. Special editions, including personalized covers, excerpts of existing books, and corporate imprints, can be created in large quantities for special needs. For more information, write to Random House, Inc., Special Markets/ Premium Sales, 1745 Broadway, MD 6-2, New York, NY, 10019 or e-mail specialmarkets@randomhouse.com.

Library of Congress Cataloging-in-Publication Data is available.

Visit the Random House Reference Web site: www.randomwords.com

Printed in the United States of America

10 9 8 7 6 5 4 3 2 1

ISBN: 0-375-721266

TABLE OF CONTENTS

PART III: **Adventure/Competition Shows** 87

INTRODUCTION

With well over one hundred shows, 10 million regular viewers, and $50 million in prize money up for grabs, reality TV has quickly become America's fast track to celebrity, wealth, and even true love. Thanks to reality TV, we now live in a world where every John or Jane Doe has the opportunity to realize his or her fifteen minutes of fame—a world where young, bratty heiresses can become famous simply by *remaining* young, bratty heiresses; where ordinary people can win millions of dollars by outwitting and outlasting total strangers on a tropical island or in a race around the world; and where naive young kids can become pop icons even if they sing really, really poorly.

How did this happen?

For children of the 1980s such as myself, the term "reality TV" is relatively new. In fact, I don't remember hearing it until the late 1990s, sometime between the Clinton sex scandal and Y2K debacle. Until then, "reality-based programming" would have meant only one thing to me: game shows.

But although the genre didn't have a name until recently, the truth is that reality TV has existed in many forms for many years. *Candid Camera*, for example—now considered the first reality television show—debuted in 1949. Similarly, 1956 saw the debut of the Jack Bailey-hosted *Queen for a Day*: the first reality TV "weepie." The roots of such family-centered shows as MTV's *The Osbournes* can be traced to the 1973 Reality classic *An American Family*. And 1976 brought us *The Gong Show* with Chuck Barris, of whom I think fondly during each audition episode of *American Idol.*

During the last five years, a great deal of attention has been paid to the cultural implications of reality television. Many regard the genre as a harbinger of the apocalypse; indeed, it seems that each new reality show causes someone (often me) to mutter under his breath, "Well, now they've really done it. This is the end of days for sure. Are those hooves I hear?" So is reality TV a sign, or even a symptom, of our times? Is its proliferation a sign that we are deteriorating as a culture?

Not so much. Then why, all of a sudden, is reality TV popping up everywhere? Why can a person not watch prime-time TV without seeing the guy who served him coffee this morning eating a vat of worms in the hopes of winning $50,000 (a thing that actually happened to me)?

The easy answer? Reality TV is cost-effective. An entire season of an average reality TV show costs about as much as just one or two episodes of, say, *ER*, which is why networks are able to take more chances with reality TV programming and produce a greater number of shows. This wasn't true in the pre-digital era. Indeed, thirty years ago it was more expensive to take a television crew on the road than it was to shoot a program in-studio. Today, however, it takes only about $50,000 worth of camera and sound equipment to shoot a reality TV show comparable to what you might see tonight on prime time. In today's era of camcorders and cell phone cameras, an episode of reality TV costs less than a music video to produce. The good news, then, is that the rise of reality TV is simple math, not the coming of the Four Horsemen: In the technologically progressive times in which we live, reality TV makes good economic sense. And, perhaps more important, these shows are just plain entertaining.

So now that there are more reality TV shows than ever, how can *you* tap into the reality-TV craze? The reality of reality TV is that producers of the average reality show select less than 5 percent of the sometimes tens of thousands of hopefuls who apply for a spot on their show each season. How can *you* get a leg up on the competition?

That's where this book comes in. I believe it to be my job—nay, my duty—to help you get on the reality TV show of your dreams. In this book, for the first time, readers are invited backstage, into the inner workings of reality television, to find out exactly how contestants and cast members are chosen, the hoops through which they are required to jump, and what tricks of the trade can better prepare them for a reality TV audition.

I began my research for this book with nothing but a deep-seated love of reality TV, a photographic memory of its every televised moment, a handful of entertainment-world connections, and the will to help the American people better their chances at getting cast on their favorite reality shows. I thought I knew everything about reality TV, but I had no idea how deep the rabbit hole actually was.

Like the star of a *Mission Impossible* episode gone awry, I infiltrated every single reality-TV production company in Los Angeles to interview reality-TV casting agents. During my research, I experienced firsthand every single facet of the reality-TV casting process. I interviewed over fifty reality-TV casting agents, attended live tapings, visited sets, attended countless open calls, partied with dozens of cast members, auditioned for a handful of shows, and even got cast and appeared on a reality TV show myself. (I'm contractually unable to reveal the name of the show on which I was cast, and I had to change my name in order to appear on it. It's a dating show, it's on cable, and that's all I can say.) At this point, there is no one in the world who knows more about reality TV than I do. And neither I nor reality TV will ever be the same.

The twenty-five reality shows covered in this book were chosen based on their consistent popularity and/or contribution to the world of reality-TV auditioning. I believe this book covers the gamut of reality-TV auditioning processes and should therefore be of use to all prospective reality-TV auditioners long past the time many of these shows have come and gone. I've broken this book down into what I deem to be the five food groups of Reality TV: Social-Experiment, Makeover/Renovation, Adventure/Competition, Dating/Romance and Talent-Based. If you don't find the show you're looking for, figure out what food group your show falls into and then read through that whole section. If I've done my job (and I believe I have) you should find all the tips and strategies necessary to get onto any reality show that could fall into that category.

Enjoy and good luck.

Matthew Robinson

PART I

Social-Experiment Shows

"It wasn't not funny!"
-Tammy, *Real World: Los Angeles*

Social-experiment reality shows offer no money or prizes to participants, and are cast with "normal" people rather than celebrities. They are the docudramas of reality TV.

THE REAL WORLD

STAT SHEET

PREMISE:
"This is the true story of seven strangers, picked to live in a house and have their lives taped, and find out what happens when people stop being polite and start getting real."

HOST:
None

NETWORK:
MTV

YEARS RUNNING:
Season 1 (New York) first aired in 1992.
Season 16 (Austin) will begin airing in 2005.

CONTACT:
Bunim/Murray—Phone: (818) 754-5790
Web: *www.bunim-murray.com*

PRODUCTION COMPANY:
Bunim/Murray (the company that brought you such shows as *Road Rules*, *The Simple Life*, *Starting Over*, and *Making the Band 2*)

EXECUTIVE PRODUCERS:
Jonathan Murray, Mary-Ellis Bunim
(passed away in 2004)

CONTESTANT AGE RANGE:
18–26

NUMBER OF APPLICANTS EACH SEASON:
35,000

NUMBER OF CONTESTANTS CHOSEN:
Seven per season

The Audition Process

If you're not familiar with *The Real World*, you've either been living under a rock or you're my grandmother (in which case, hi Nana, I love you!). But if you're like most of us, you've seen it, you know it, you love it. And you want on.

The *Real World* casting process—widely dubbed the "Bunim/Murray casting process" after the producers who devised it—is imitated by nearly every other reality show in one way or another. It is the most original and respected casting process in the business: the mold from which all other casting processes are cast (pun intended). To put it simply: *The Real World* invented the game.

Since the *Real World* brand name is so well known, the show's producers don't have to do any street recruiting. That means you're gonna have to go to them. There are two ways onto the show: submission of a mailed-in videotape or a visit to an open casting call. The show attracts around thirty-five thousand applicants each season—about two thousand applicants per open call and fifteen thousand videotapes—but don't let those numbers daunt you. The casting process is designed to let the brightest personalities shine, so if you're right for the show, you'll have your chance to prove it. Let's start with the open calls.

Open Casting Calls

You can pretty much bet the farm (but please, don't really bet your farm) that a new *Real World* season will be cast every twelve months. The months and cities in which the show casts vary from year to year, so don't despair if you live in Des Moines: The show just may be coming your way this year. Your best bet is to check the Bunim/Murray Web site at *www.bunim-murray.com* for exact dates and locations of casting calls. Although the production company does advertise the details of these calls on the radio, in newspapers, and in fliers handed out on college campuses, the only proactive way to ensure the producers meet you face-to-face is to check the Web.

Casting-wise, Jonathan Murray and Mary-Ellis Bunim are most famous for inventing a unique version of the open casting call. Their system, the "ten-people-talking-at-a-table" system, is widely copied by other reality shows. It is their "secret sauce," if you will: the signature ingredient that ensures they get the best possible batch of people from their casting process each season. Here's how it works.

At the open call, expect to see a long line filled with attractive people. Be prepared to wait. More important, be prepared to talk. There's no better opportunity to stand out as a type A personality than in the line at the open call. The reason is this: Even though the casting directors will be running around like crazy people, they'll also be watching you out of the corners of their eyes (but not in a creepy way). Plus, the people with whom you're waiting might very well be the same people with whom you'll be grouped at the casting call. Get to know them, get comfortable with them, find out their names, and let them know who you are.

Before you enter the main casting room (often a tent set up in a parking lot), you'll have to fill out a one-page form indicating your name, address, occupation, and other basic information. Then the casting directors will take a Polaroid picture of you. Once this is completed, they'll lead you into the casting room. (Cue tense music.)

You'll be brought in and seated at a table with ten other people—most likely the people who stood in front of and behind you in line. If you've done your homework, you'll already know the group dynamic here: what each person is like, who has the strongest type A personality, and so on.

A casting director is assigned to each table, and he or she will ask your group a few questions in order to inspire some conversation. That sounds easy, but there's a catch. The questions are designed to provoke very strong answers from people—for example, "How do you feel about abortion?"; "What do you think about affirmative action?"; or "How do you feel about women using their sexuality to get ahead in the business world?" The casting director will direct these questions to the entire table, then simply sit back and watch what happens. Casting directors will not join in on the conversation themselves; if the conversation lulls, they'll simply ask another question.

The aim of this exercise is not so much to rile you up as to find out who's the most vocal, the most confident, the most interesting, and the most self-assured personality at the table—all in ten minutes or less. That's right: You'll be finished with this phase of the casting call in ten minutes or less. And as if that isn't fast enough, most casting directors worth their salt say they can spot a keeper within the first thirty seconds.

If the casting directors like you, they'll instruct an intern to tap you discreetly on the shoulder and ask you to stick around a while longer. You'll be asked to fill out a sixteen-page application that delves a little deeper into your life than the one-pager you filled out while waiting in line; questions will address such topics as your love life, family life, work life, and childhood. I've been told it takes about an hour and a half to complete, and that the producers will allow you to take it home or back to work with you and return it at the end of the day if you can't stick around. Once you've completed the application, the first round of the casting process is over.

Video Application

If you can't make it to an open casting call, it's time to get out your video camera and make a five-to-ten-minute movie. Any consumer video format is acceptable (VHS, Hi8, 8mm, VHS-C, mini-DV, etc.), and there really are no rules here. On its Web site, Bunim/Murray asks for a straight sit-down interview, but I was told by the casting directors that a little creativity never hurt anyone, just as long as the "real you" shines through. While most people simply sit in front of the camera and talk about themselves, others take viewers on a tour of their world—introducing their parents, significant others, etc. The only thing the casting directors don't really care about is your pet: Leave Sparky out of it.

What follows is a list of Bunim/Murray's official tips for your video application. Though most of these tips may seem insignificant, observing them could easily mean the difference between making a video that gets passed along to the casting directors and making one that gets thrown out.

SEND YOUR TAPE TO:

★★★★★★★★★★★★★★★★★★★★

The Real World Casting
Bunim/Murray Productions
6007 Sepulveda Blvd
Van Nuys, CA 91411

★★★★★★★★★★★★★★★★★★★★

Don't forget to include a piece of paper listing your name, age, phone number, address, and E-mail address (if you have one).

★ Make sure the auto-focus feature on your camera is turned off, or the image in your video will blur every time you move.

★ Make sure the room in which you film your video is bright enough for you to be seen, but not *too* bright.

★ Make sure there is no date/time stamp on the picture in your video.

★ Don't sit too far away from the camera. Four feet from the camera is about the right distance. But no closer than that—the casting directors want to see your whole head and shoulders.

★ Keep it quiet in the background. No music or TV (you crazy kids).

Bunim/Murray looks at every single tape that it receives. Even if it's just a tape of you sleeping or picking your nose, someone will watch it (though probably on fast-forward). Better yet, the people watching these tapes aren't interns and production assistants, as is the case with many shows. All the tapes are watched by actual members of the casting team. So let your personality win them over, be yourself, and have fun!

Round Two and Beyond

If you receive a phone call after completing either of the previous tasks, you're probably one of a thousand people selected from among thirty-five thousand applicants—not bad! From this point on here's what you can expect:

If you live in the Los Angeles area, Bunim/Murray will ask you to visit its production offices for an interview. If you don't live near Los Angeles, casting directors will conduct the same interview over the phone. Though it may seem odd, you'll be asked to talk on speakerphone and to film yourself on the phone during the interview. Bet you've never done that before.

There are no "typical" questions asked during these interviews; rather, questions will generally relate to topics you mentioned in your long application—for example, "What's going on with your boyfriend/girlfriend?" or "You said you had a tough childhood, tell me some more about that." There are no right or wrong answers here; rather, the casting directors want to get a feel for how you react during a filmed one-on-one conversation.

WHAT THEY'RE LOOKING FOR

The party line among the casting team at Bunim/Murray is that it's looking for people who can't help but be themselves. Type A personalities. People who are always the center of attention. People who speak their mind. Big personalities. These are the phrases the *Real World* casting team repeatedly invokes. There is no room for shy or quiet people on *The Real World* because, for the most part, such people will only become shyer and quieter when surrounded by type A personalities.

In reality, however, it's not always as simple as it sounds. Bunim/Murray has to cast *The Real World* with diversity in mind. One casting director explained to me that each season of *The Real World* is like a puzzle: You have to find the correct combination of seven people, all of whom connect to each other and create a good picture. The result, she told me, is that countless auditioners each season are perfect for *The Real World*, but not for that particular season or cast. But have no fear: The casting team almost always calls those people back the next year to try again, and a few of these callbacks have even resulted in casting!

Like I always say: Be yourself, but be prepared, and make sure to bring your "A" game whenever you're in a casting situation. Keep it "realer" than the rest, and you just might end up on *The Real World*—the original king of reality TV shows.

You may be asked to conduct up to four or five of these interviews before you make it to the finals. But each time you do another interview, know that you're moving up one more level on the casting pyramid.

Real World finalists constitute less than 1 percent of the original auditioners— fewer than fifty people. As a finalist, you will be flown to Los Angeles, put up in a hotel, and interviewed ad nauseum. Over a week or two, the casting team will do everything it can to get to know you better. Along the way, you'll meet with Jonathan Murray and the rest of the Bunim/Murray executives. Finalists will be eliminated until only seven strangers remain, waiting to move into their house. Hopefully one of them will be you.

Did You Know?

Puck of *The Real World: San Francisco*, probably the most infamous *Real World* cast member to date, was the only member of any *Real World* cast to be unanimously kicked out of the house. Other *Real World*-ers forced to vacate their homes prematurely include David from *The Real World: Los Angeles* and Ruby from *The Real World: Hawaii*.

Interview
Amaya Bruescher, *The Real World: Hawaii*

MR: Tell me how you first heard that *The Real World* was casting.

AB: I actually had no idea about the casting. I was home in the Bay Area visiting my family. My best friend and I were contemplating what to do that day. We were on the freeway, we were going to go to Berkeley, and at the last minute we decided to go to San Francisco.

We were walking through San Francisco and we saw a line outside Planet Hollywood and we were like, "I bet that's for *The Real World* auditions." We started walking away when both of us got this bizarre feeling in our stomachs about halfway down the block. We were both like, "Do you feel weird? I feel weird." We turned around and said, "We have nothing better to do. Let's go stand in line."

So I stood in line, filled out the questionnaire. I just thought the whole thing was hilarious. Next thing I knew I was sitting at a table with my best friend, a couple of other people, and the casting people, and I was just answering the questions they asked me honestly, not thinking anything was going to happen.

MR: What were they asking you?

AB: Where I went to school, what my major was, did I live in the dorms, friendships and family. When it was over, I got up, and I thought I was done. My best friend and I were walking away when one of the casting girls came running after us and pulled us back to have a talk with Mary-Ellis Bunim, the producer.

Again it was a table discussion, same kind of stuff: "Tell me about growing up. Is there anything you've had to struggle with?" I just began answering questions honestly.

The next morning I got a call, and they told me to make a ten-minute tape. I was still at home—I hadn't lived at home for years. I had to quickly find a video camera. My best friend directed me. I talked for ten minutes about who I was, where I was at that point in my life, how I felt about things.

MR: What types of things did you say?

AB: Well, here's the thing. I was doing an interview in my childhood bedroom, which I hadn't lived in for almost four years. I was like, "I'm here in this room, giving this interview, which is weird because this room represents kind of an old part of me, but there's a whole new part of me now."

I showed them a picture of my sorority, and explained that I didn't really fit in, and I just talked about what I did in school and what I thought the *Real World* experience would offer me.

I've always been a person who said, "What the hell, I'll try it." That's why I joined a sorority in the first place, because I was like, "I don't know anything about sororities, I'll go through rush!" And I ended up in one of the best houses on campus. Things happen to me.

Funny thing is, I wasn't supposed to be on *Real World*. I was going to be on *Road Rules*. In fact, I asked to be on *Road Rules*, because it was *Semester at Sea* and they went to so many countries, and I thought it sounded more fun to travel.

MR: What was the casting process like?

AB: The casting process was very long, very in-depth. I treated it as therapy. I just spilled my guts; I told them everything. I cried once when the process dealt with stuff about my dad. Throughout the whole process, I was like, "There's no way I'm going to get this." But they kept calling me back.

I never really thought anything was going to happen. In fact, I was pissed when I was called and told that I got it, because I was like, "I could have taken a few extra courses and breezed through my senior year, but now I'm on *The Real World*!"

MR: What do you think helped you get on _The Real World_?

AB: I think having a weird name helped me a lot. I know it's really bizarre, but it's true. If you have a weird name it gets you farther, because it makes you stand out from everyone else. People remember your name because it's so weird, and then they start remembering things about your personality. It's funny, but a strange name really helps.

MR: How long was the whole casting process?

AB: About four months.

MR: Were you excited when you got on?

AB: I was like, "What am I doing?" When I got cast I felt extremely lonely, and I felt that way pretty much until the show aired and the whole thing was over.

MR: Why?

AB: It's a scary process. And what they do to you afterwards is another thing. You have to deal with the chaos, people screaming your name. I think because I have brown hair and bangs now, people won't recognize me, but it still happens every day. I lived with some messed-up people, so it just wasn't an easy experience.

When I think back on it, I hate that year. I won't even drink a bottle of wine from 1999, I don't even want to hear that song; 1999 was, like, my lowest point. But just because it was low doesn't mean it was a bad thing. From adversity comes change. I was twenty-one then; I was young.

MR: How do you feel you were portrayed on the show? Did they capture the "real" you?

AB: They captured a little bit of me, but they got none of my humor, none of my intellect.

They played up my old eating disorder to make it fill a whole episode. I think that was the most irresponsible move that they could have made. They took a recovering person with an eating disorder who was very proud of her success, and they turned that around and used it against me. I thought that was really mean.

Sometimes they got some of my humor, but I wish they got me more. I was really great friends with the crew. By the end of it I really got along well with them, even though we weren't supposed to talk.

MR: What advice would you give someone who wanted to be on reality TV?

AB: Be the most real version of yourself. I associate being myself with John Cougar Mellencamp's "Authority Song." When I'm alone in my house, sometimes I blast that song and dance around like an idiot. That's what they need to see on your tape. Also, if your personality involves some kind of dichotomy, they love that. Or if you're a person on the verge of discovering themselves. They want you in flux, they want your transition.

I say just be the best version of yourself, and not a fake version. And if you're an alcoholic, admit it. And if you're a huge, bland, all-American guy, you're probably going to do well.

Also, be prepared to lose your anonymity and to not necessarily look like yourself. There are people who will write a script and make you a character. Then you become that character to the general viewing public, and that's who you will be for probably the next five to ten years. I mean, look at Becky from *The Real World: New York*. Fifteen years later, she's still getting recognized. You will get harassed, people will find you, and you will get talked about at your high school reunion.

And lastly, don't get involved with somebody on your cast, because you'll be a guinea pig and you'll be known as part of "Colin and Amaya" for the rest of your life.

MR: Are there any good reasons to be on reality TV?

AB: If you want to be famous. If you want to experience things that most people don't usually get to experience. I got to go skydiving. I went to India. I've been able to get in places and do things I might not have been able to do. I speak at colleges, and it's given me the ability to talk about a subject that's near and dear to me: eating disorders.

You can take the visibility and do something great with it, or you can do something bad with it. You can also successfully disappear back into normal life. If you're a guy, you can grow a beard. If you're a chick, you can change your hair color, which might or might not work. But it is possible to do reality TV and become a functioning member of society again.

Basically, you're talking to someone who went through something crazy who is now trying to be a normal person. I'm trying to be like Dominic from *The Real World: Los Angeles*. I saw him at Mary-Ellis's (the producer's) funeral, and I have to say I was almost starstruck because he's one of those guys who did the show and you never heard from him again.

SOME TIPS FROM AMAYA ON "HOW TO KEEP *THE REAL WORLD* REAL":

★ ★ ★ ★ ★ ★ ★ ★ ★ ★ ★ ★ ★ ★ ★ ★ ★ ★ ★ ★

1. Change your hair color in the middle of the season, because then the producers will have to present your experience chronologically.

2. Swear a lot, because the producers can't use footage in which you're swearing, and it's very costly for them to "bleep" profanity.

3. Go naked, because it costs a lot of money to pixelate your private parts.

4. Sing a song by The Beatles, because it costs Bunim/Murray five thousand dollars to license each song.

Amaya Bruescher currently lives and works in Los Angeles, California.

★ ★ ★ ★ ★ ★ ★ ★ ★ ★ ★ ★ ★ ★ ★ ★ ★ ★ ★ ★

STAT SHEET

PREMISE:
What happens when two completely different families trade a family member for an entire week?

HOST:
None

NETWORK:
FOX

YEARS RUNNING:
Season 1 ran from 2004 to 2005. Season 2 will begin airing in 2005.

CONTACT:
Rocket Science—Phone: (323) 802-0500
Web: *www.fox.com/tradingspouses/*

PRODUCTION COMPANY:
Rocket Science (the company that brought you such shows as *Joe Millionaire*, *My Big Fat Obnoxious Fiancé*, *Temptation Island*, and *Renovate My Family*)

EXECUTIVE PRODUCERS:
Chris Cowan, Jean-Michel Michenaud

CONTESTANT AGE RANGE:
All ages

NUMBER OF APPLICANTS EACH SEASON:
10,000 families

NUMBER OF CONTESTANTS CHOSEN:
Two families per show (number of family members varies), 12–15 episodes per season

TRADING SPOUSES

As titillating as it sounds, *Trading Spouses* is actually a sweet tearjerker in which families learn to appreciate each other by seeing what one another's seemingly "opposite" lives are like. In a typical episode, producers take a strict, well-organized mom and toss her into a messy, "wild" mom's household to see what happens. Usually the clean mom learns to relax a bit, the wild mom learns to clean up more often, both moms flee back to their families with renewed love and excitement, and the audience sheds a few tears. Not bad for a FOX show.

The Audition Process

There are two ways to be cast on *Trading Spouses*: attending an open casting call or applying on the show's Web site.

Open Casting Calls

The most effective way to get cast on *Trading Spouses*, as is the case with many audition scenarios, is to show up in person at an open casting call with your family in tow. Make sure you bring pictures of your family members, both individually and as a group, as well as *extensive* photos of your house, inside and out. (And be sure to know the square footage of your house!)

So, where can you find these open casting calls? Generally, casting calls are only held in cities that casting directors deem "hot": Atlanta, Boston, Dallas, Los Angeles, New York, Chicago, or Las Vegas.

If you live in one of these cities, be on the lookout for the show's producers publicizing a casting call in your area—the most common types of publicity are radio spots, classified ads in the local newspaper, postings on Web sites such as *www.craigslist.org*, and fliers distributed at malls, fairs, and other crowded venues. In particular, the casting team loves to hit family-oriented spots such as Home Depot and Chuck E. Cheese, so keep your eyes open. You can also check the FOX Web site (*www.fox.com*) for updated casting information.

Once you find out about the open call, get your family down there as early as possible on the appointed day. The casting director told me that hundreds, if not thousands, of families show up to these open casting calls, so be prepared to wait for three hours or more.

Once your name is called, you'll meet with the show's recruiters. They'll ask you a few questions—for example, why you think *your* family should be on *Trading Spouses*, and how you would best describe your family. They'll take some photos and take down your family's general information—phone number, address, etc.— and that will be it.

Applying Online

If you don't live in one of the "hot" cities and you can't get to an open casting call, the Internet may be your best bet. Head over to *www.fox.com/tradingspouses* and find the appropriate link (it should read something along the lines of "*Trading*

Spouses is now casting! Click here for details!"), or try *www.tradingspousescasting.com*, which isn't always up, but is worth a shot. Whichever Web site you visit, here's what it will tell you to do:

As long as you're a legal resident of the U.S. and your children are five years of age or older, send an E-mail to *apply@tradingspouses.com* with the following information:

1. The names and ages of your family members

2. Your family's contact information (including address)

3. A brief description of your family and its members. Explain what makes you interesting and why you want to be on the show.

4. Pictures of your entire family, attached in JPEG format.

   Assemble your E-mail and click "send." That's it. The rest of the process will be the same for all applicants, regardless of whether they applied through an open casting call or the Web site.

Round Two and Beyond

If the casting directors like your application, they'll call you and conduct a phone interview. During the phone interview, the casting team will essentially take on the role of your therapist in the hopes of getting as much dirt (aka potential TV drama) out of you as possible. If they find you riveting, they'll send a full camera crew to your house. And when I say "full," I mean *really full*, so be prepared.

The crew will film every inch of your home, conduct private interviews with each family member (more dirt-digging), and try to get a feel for how your family members interact with each other.

WHAT THEY'RE LOOKING FOR

Everyone thinks he or she has the greatest family ever. Everyone thinks it would be hilarious to watch his or her family switch places with an alter-ego family. Most likely, however, for the purposes of *Trading Spouses*, your family wouldn't be that entertaining to the American viewing public. And when I say that, I mean no offense to your family. On the contrary, you should take it as a compliment: it means your family is too multi-faceted for the often one-dimensional world of reality TV. Most families are.

First off, if you have a small family—if, for example, you're an only child—chances are good that the show won't be interested. I'm not saying that small families shouldn't apply, just that they might have a smaller chance of success with this particular show. Generally, *Trading Spouses* wants the "typical" family, the kind of family with 2.5 kids and a dog.

In fact, let's take this opportunity to state the Golden Rule of *Trading Spouses* casting: If you can't classify your family as a specific *type* of family—for example, the Messy Family, the Obsessive-Compulsive family, the American-as-Apple-Pie Family, the Packrat Family, the Dysfunctional Family, the Loud-and-Obnoxious Family, the Creepy-Quiet-Dinners Family—then neither can the casting director, and your family won't get cast. It's true that every family is messy or dysfunctional or obsessive-compulsive *sometimes*. But is your family *always* this way? If so, *Trading Spouses* is your show.

The reason for the Golden Rule? In order to pit two families against one another and have it create lots of TV-worthy drama, the families need to be *extremely* different. Each family needs to be larger-than-life, so that when it clashes with the other larger-than-life family, things *really* get interesting. In short, the casting team needs a "hook" when it pitches the episode to the network. Nobody wants to watch an episode titled "Reasonably Happy Family vs. Relatively

Normal Family." But *everybody* wants to watch "The Munster Family vs. The Squeaky-Clean Family."

The bottom line: You've got to be extreme, and you've got to be some other family's opposite.

And whatever your family's "angle"—whatever "personality" you sold to the casting team in your application—keep in mind that every family member will need to stick to that personality in order to make it on the show. Don't be afraid to amp things up a bit. Crank up the volume on your larger-than-life family to "10"—maybe even to "11." Remember that *Trading Spouses* isn't interested in the individual personalities of your family members; instead, it wants to make your family unit a single character with a single extreme personality. And so, youngest to oldest, you've all got to sell your part.

In particular, the member of your family who will trade places with a member of the alter-ego family must act as the perfect representative for your family and its personality. Remember, this is a show about the *trading* of family members. As such, the producers are not looking for drama within your own family so much as they're looking for drama that someone in your family would create if they were thrown into an alter-ego family's camp.

Finally, keep in mind that your family can't be depressing—at least, not the type of depressing that can't be made "un-depressing" in under an hour. No incurable diseases, no history of abuse, no "my house was destroyed by a tornado." There are plenty of other shows for you if you fall into one of these categories; *Trading Spouses* just ain't one of them.

And when all else fails, just be yourself and hope it's exactly what the casting directors are looking for. They gotta pick someone.

The camera crew's footage will then be sent back to the casting directors, who will edit the footage into five-minute presentations for the show's producers. If the producers like you, they'll present you to the network for consideration. If the network likes you, then you're in.

After you've been accepted by the network, the only remaining obstacles are a series of evaluations for you and your family members: three medical examinations by three different doctors, psychological evaluations by an armada of psychologists, and an in-depth background check by private investigators of everything each member of your family has done since the day he or she was born.

Easy, right?

Did You Know?

For the first season of *Trading Spouses* ten separate families made it to the final auditioning round, went through all of the medical and psychological tests and prepared their houses for filming only to be disqualified when the producers found out that a member of each of the families had lied about doing time behind bars. Ten separate families! Who are all these jailbirds trying to get on TV?

PART II

Makeover/Renovation Shows

"We're not here to change you,
we're here to make you better."
-Carson Kressley, *Queer Eye for the Straight Guy*

Makeover shows form the time-tested cornerstone of reality television.
Home- and car-themed fixer-upper shows have extended the genre beyond its original
foundation of personal-makeover shows.

EXTREME
MAKEOVER

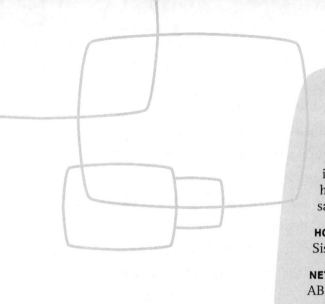

STAT SHEET

PREMISE:
Deserving and long-suffering
individuals receive life-transforming
head-to-toe makeovers. (The name
says it all!)

HOST:
Sissy Biggers (season 1); Sam Saboura (season 2–)

NETWORK:
ABC

YEARS RUNNING:
Season 1 first aired in December 2002.

CONTACT:
Web: *abc.go.com/primetime/extrememakeover/*

PRODUCTION COMPANY:
Greengrass Productions

EXECUTIVE PRODUCER:
Howard Schultz

CONTESTANT AGE RANGE:
21 and over

NUMBER OF APPLICANTS EACH SEASON:
30,000

NUMBER OF CONTESTANTS CHOSEN:
Two per episode, 12–15 episodes
per season

Extreme Makeover debuted in 2002, the first in a long line of shock-laden "total makeover" shows to hit the airwaves in recent years. Three seasons later, it's still as popular as ever. Those lucky enough to get cast on *Extreme Makeover* won't have to settle for your average new-wardrobe-and-a-dye-job makeover. No, no, no — there would be nothing extreme about that. *Extreme Makeover* cast members can expect to have their noses broken, their faces reconfigured, their

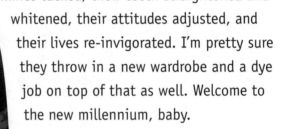

tummies tucked, their teeth straightened and whitened, their attitudes adjusted, and their lives re-invigorated. I'm pretty sure they throw in a new wardrobe and a dye job on top of that as well. Welcome to the new millennium, baby.

And its name, *Extreme Makeover*, once again proves the reality-TV theory that whichever show airs first gets to use the most obvious title. (Also, it has the best host name ever: Sissy Biggers. You just can't make this stuff up, people.)

Who wouldn't want an extreme makeover? Well, me for starters, but who cares what I think? Let's find out how to get you on that show!

The Audition Process

The only two ways to appear on *Extreme Makeover* are to attend an open casting call or send in a video application.

Open Casting Call

Check the ABC Web site at *www.abc.com* for up-to-the-minute information about the dates and locations of open calls.

When you arrive at the open call, expect to fill out a short questionnaire while you wait in line. Although it's not necessary, it's a good idea to bring a few photos of yourself to the call—preferably a close-up and a full-body shot.

The audition process for *Extreme Makeover* is an interesting one. Once you get to the front of the line, you'll be led into a small, curtained booth where you'll be directed to make a three-minute case for why you should receive an extreme makeover. There will be no casting people interviewing you: It will just be you and a camera, alone in a booth. Since the open call is so similar to the video application process, I've placed the bulk of the tips and strategies on what to say and how to say it in the sections below.

When you're done, you'll exit the booth and head on your way. In essence, the producers are simply supplying you with an opportunity to create a video application using their equipment.

Now, while I like the idea of a "confessional"-style open call, it just doesn't seem worth it to go to the trouble of traveling all the way to the audition location and waiting in line for a couple of hours, only to make the same video you could have made at home. Also, if you make your tape at home you can edit your performance or restart the tape if you make a mistake. At the live audition, you'll get only one shot.

If you don't own or have access to a video camera, then the open call is your only option—and it's a good one at that. But since there's no real difference between the two application methods, as long as you can get your hands on a video camera, I recommend submitting a video application that you make yourself.

Video Application

The same rules apply to a video application as apply to the video you would make at the open call: You get only three minutes to make your case. In addition to your three-minute confessional, you'll be asked to film close-ups of your "problem areas." (I'm not going to tell you where your "problem areas" might be, but if you're applying to be on *Extreme Makeover*, chances are good that you already know what they are.) Simply hold the camera up to these areas and film them for at least ten seconds each, just as if you were taking a photo with a regular point-and-shoot camera.

During your three-minute interview, your main goal is to communicate who you are and why you deserve an extreme makeover. It's important that you explain how your looks have affected you, and how an appearance on *Extreme Makeover* would improve your life.

Since three minutes isn't a whole lot of time, don't get too fancy with your tape. Just sit in front of the camera—make sure the lighting is right, neither too bright nor too dark—and give your spiel (i.e., "speech").

Extreme Makeover is what used to be known as a "weepie" on daytime television, which means that it's a show geared toward making women (or sensitive men) cry. Why the big sobfest? Because this show is dedicated to rebuilding the lives and bodies of people who have unusually sad stories. And I'm not talking about your basic "I-was-made-fun-of-in-school-for-my-big-nose" stories; I'm talking about *horror* stories. For example, if you had food thrown at you every day of high school, went to prom alone, got left at the altar by your fiancée for having "lizard skin," and now live in your mother's attic where you emerge only at night so you can eat in peace without people screaming "beached whale!," then you've got a story *Extreme Makeover* might be interested in. So unless you've got a life story that brings people to tears every time you tell it, *Extreme Makeover* probably won't be interested in you. Evoking emotion from the casting department is the name of the game, so do whatever you can to up the tearjerker factor. My motto for these types of shows is: "If you have a casting director crying, you have a casting director calling." (Who have I become?)

At the same time, however, don't appear so down in the dumps that you seem to lack any hope of rehabilitation. You've got to want to change your life for the better and, more important, you've got to believe it's possible. While plastic surgery will certainly make you *look* different, you're not going to give the

SEND YOUR TAPE TO:

★ ★

Once you're happy with your tape (which must be VHS, mini-DV, Hi8, or VHS-C format), label it with your name and region number (as indicated below). Download the show's application from the ABC Web site, fill it out completely, and send the whole package to:

★ ★

Extreme Makeover [Region Number]
10061 Riverside Drive
Toluca Lake, CA 91602

★ ★

From the following list, find the city closest to you and use the corresponding number as the region number on your tape and envelope.

01. New York, NY	*07. Louisville, KY*
02. Baltimore, MD	*08. St. Louis, MO*
03. Orlando, FL	*09. Dallas, TX*
04. Atlanta, GA	*10. Denver, CO*
05. Indianapolis, IN	*11. Seattle, WA*
06. Minneapolis, MN	*12. Los Angeles, CA*

The city corresponding to your region number is the city you will be asked to visit for your second-round interview, at your own expense, should you be called back.

producers the story arc they're looking for unless you can also experience an *emotional* transformation on the show.

If you can incorporate all of the above into a speech and say it in under three minutes, whether at home or at an open call, you'll be on the right track to getting cast on *Extreme Makeover*.

Round Two and Beyond

An extended interview and a giant application await you if you're invited to participate in the second round of the casting process. Expect a thirty-minute taped interview delving deep into your past, your self-image, and your dreams of what an extreme makeover could do for you.

If they like you, the casting department will use your taped interview to pitch you to the show's producers and to network executives. If you are selected to be on the show, expect a full week of filming and four to seven weeks of rehabilitation, followed by a few days of additional filming once your "transformation" is complete. That's a lot of sick days to cash in at work, so make sure this is something you really want to do before you advance to this point in the audition process.

Did You Know?

Sissy Biggers, the original host of *Extreme Makeover*, got her start on cooking shows such as *Ready Set Cook* and *Iron Chef USA*. Who says baking a pie is all that different from reconstructive surgery?

WHAT THEY'RE LOOKING FOR

I said before: the casting directors at *Extreme Makeover* want horror stories. The worse a person looks and the harder his or her life has been, the more amazing the transformation will seem when he or she emerges as a happy and beautiful person at the end of the hour-long episode. Not to be harsh, but if mirrors don't shatter when you walk by them, and if people don't sob when you tell them your life story, you may not be "extreme" enough for *Extreme Makeover*.

The flip side is that, in addition to communicating to the casting team all the pain you've endured, you've also got to show that life hasn't crushed your spirit or stifled your optimism. The show's producers want to inspire America with amazing stories of personal transformation and rebirth, not dishearten viewers with depressing tales of woe. So even though your story needs to be unusually sad, you also need to come off as hopeful and positive.

It's a tall order, I know. But that's why only a handful of people each year get picked to receive one of these $100,000 makeovers. The producers are very picky about whom they put on their show. And for the amount of money they're spending on each makeover, I don't blame them.

EXTREME MAKEOVER: HOME EDITION

STAT SHEET

PREMISE:
Designers completely renovate a deserving family's home—from top to bottom—in just seven days.

HOST:
Ty Pennington

NETWORK:
ABC

YEARS RUNNING:
First aired in December 2002

CONTACT:
Web: *abc.go.com/primetime/xtremehome/show.html*

PRODUCTION COMPANIES:
Endemol Productions, Lock and Key Productions

EXECUTIVE PRODUCERS:
Craig Armstrong, Denise Cramsey, Tom Forman

CONTESTANT AGE RANGE:
All ages

NUMBER OF APPLICANTS PER SEASON:
15,000 families

NUMBER OF CONTESTANTS CHOSEN:
One family per episode, 12–15 episodes

If you like the idea of an extreme makeover but think it would be better suited to your house than to your body, why not apply for a spot on the award-winning *Extreme Makeover: Home Edition*? They'll tear down your house, build you a bigger, better one, and help you get your life back in order all in seven days. But just like on the original *Extreme Makeover*, you've got a better chance at getting cast if you NEED the makeover rather than if you WANT it.

The Audition Process

The good news is that *Extreme Makeover: Home Edition* uses what is called a "rolling" application process, which means the show is *always* accepting applications. The only catch is that the show usually casts in different cities each season, so you'll need to check the Web site to see whether the casting team will be looking for families in your neck of the woods this time around.

Since it's kind of hard to bring your house with you to an open call, video applications are the name of the game on *Extreme Makeover: Home Edition.* So head to the Web site, download the application, break out your video camera, and get to work.

Video Application

The casting team at *Extreme Makeover: Home Edition* asks that you adhere to a fairly specific format in your video application. The reason is that, as much as they might otherwise enjoy a little creativity, they'll most likely use the application video in your episode if you're cast on the show, so it will need to look a certain way in case this happens. They also prefer that you provide them with multiple takes in each section of your video. So if you make a mistake while shooting, don't rewind and record over it—just do it again and leave both versions on the tape. Should you make it onto the show, the producers will want to have as much footage of you as possible from which to choose.

Begin the video with your entire family standing outside of your house saying in unison "Hello, ABC, we're the ____ family!" With big smiles and a wave, each member of your family should then introduce himself or herself and give his or her age. Unless you have a friend who has nominated your family to be on the show, don't include people who are not members of your family in your video. Your wacky neighbor has no place on this particular show.

Next, move inside and give a thorough tour of your house, with each member of the family giving a walk-through of his or her individual room. The most comfortable speaker in the family should give a tour of the communal rooms. The person speaking to the camera should never be operating the camera, so either pass the camera off from one family member to the next as you shoot the video, or get a friend from outside the family to film the entire thing.

Throughout your tour, make sure to incorporate your family's unique story. Explain what has happened to your house and your family, why you desperately need a renovation, and how an extreme makeover would change your family's life.

Your video should also include one long tour of the house, both inside and out, without commentary, so the show's producers can get a good feel for its layout and exterior. Provide a 360-degree view of your front yard, including nearby houses, so the crew can begin to figure out the logistics of filming in your neighborhood.

Finally, end the same way you began: with your entire family standing outside of the house, waving and smiling. In unison, say "Goodbye, ABC! We hope you pick us!" (or something along those lines).

While your tape shouldn't be ridiculously long, there's no limit as to how long it can be. It's up to you to keep the video entertaining and emotionally engaging; as long as you do this, the length of your tape won't matter.

The goal is to sell the casting team on how desperately your family needs a home renovation, so never say anything like "Our house isn't *that* bad." Your house needs to be *exactly* that bad, so play up every "problem area" you can find, and amp up the emotion in your story whenever possible.

Round Two and Beyond

Out of the fifteen thousand families who apply each season to *Extreme Makeover: Home Edition*, fewer than a hundred families make it this far. After pitching you to the show's producers, the casting team will make a few follow-up calls before coming to your house to see it, and your family, for themselves. When they come to see you, make sure to be the same family you were in your videotape. If you were energetic and peppy, make sure the casting team sees that when they arrive. Also, it's a home makeover show, so don't clean up your house for them. The messier and more desperate it looks, the more they'll want to renovate it for you. After that, as long your family passes the required medical and psychological tests, and as long as your background check reveals that no one's committed a felony, you could end up receiving an amazing home makeover!

Did You Know?

Not only will the wonderful people at *Extreme Makeover: Home Edition* build you a brand new house, but they will cover any and all new homeowner taxes you incur resulting from your property's increased value. Nifty!

WHAT THEY'RE LOOKING FOR

Extreme Makeover: Home Edition looks for families in dire situations, desperately in need of help. Therefore, only certain families and houses are eligible for casting. For example, the show is not interested in casting families who have bought fixer-uppers they simply can't afford to fix up, or families who have simply "outgrown" their homes, or any family with a home larger than two thousand square feet (which would be too big to renovate in seven days).

What the show *is* looking for, and I quote this directly from its casting team, are "families who have fallen victim to circumstances beyond their control." Just like its parent show, *Extreme Makeover*, *Extreme Makeover: Home Edition* looks for people with terribly sad—indeed, near tragic—reasons for deserving a makeover. Perhaps your wife has passed away, leaving you to raise a large family on your own, or a flood has devastated half of your home. Heaven forbid such woes should ever befall you, but these are exactly the types of stories *Extreme Makeover: Home Edition* is looking for. If your family really needs help, then this show might just be the place to find it.

On a side note, if you know a family whom you think would be perfect for the show, but whom you feel would never audition on its own, feel free to nominate that family yourself—as long as you get the family's permission to film its home, take photos, and fill out the application.

STAT SHEET

PREMISE:
With the help of a professional coach,
young people receive the chance to
get "made"—to break out of their shells
and become who they've always
wanted to be.

NETWORK:
MTV

YEARS RUNNING:
First aired in August 2002

CONTACT:
MTV—Web: *www.mtv.com*

CREATOR:
Bob Kusbit

EXECUTIVE PRODUCERS:
Bob Kusbit, Tony DiSanto

CONTESTANT AGE RANGE:
15–21

NUMBER OF APPLICANTS EACH SEASON:
5,000

NUMBER OF CONTESTANTS CHOSEN:
One per episode, twelve episodes per season

MADE

One of MTV's first "lifestyle makeover" shows, *Made* provides a positive, real-life look at young people's search for self. I emphasize the word "young" here because, aside from the occasional exception, *Made* centers around high school kids. Formally, the network considers applications from kids between the ages of fifteen (high school freshmen) and twenty-one (college seniors). Generally, however, the casting team selects applicants from the bottom half of that age bracket.

Made isn't a talent competition, or a chance for you to become a superstar. It's a show about overcoming life obstacles to become the person you've always wanted to be. If you're the shy girl who wants to shock everyone with her dance moves at the spring formal, or the skinny towel boy who wants to prove himself by going out for the football team, then you're the type of person who wants to get *Made*.

The Audition Process

As is the case with all MTV shows, for casting information you can visit *www.mtv.com*, click on "Shows," and then click on "Casting Call" to find out whether the show is currently casting, or for updated casting instructions.

Made is cast in two ways: from video applications or from high school open calls.

High School Open Calls

What in the name of all that is holy is a "high school open call," you ask? Well, the *Made* casting team petitions a high school (usually somewhere on the East Coast) for the right to hold an open call at that school, either after school hours or during lunch. If Mr. or Ms. Principal gives MTV the A-OK, then MTV sends home permission slips with every interested member of the student body. If you can convince your parents to sign the form, which gives MTV the right to interview and videotape you, then you will be allowed to show up at the open call.

If you're lucky enough to be a student at one of these chosen high schools, here's what you can expect. A lone member of the casting team, armed only with a camera and an inquisitive mind, will make his or her way to your school auditorium. You, along with your rowdy cohorts, will line up outside the auditorium and await your turn to enter the auditorium and "pitch" your idea to the casting person.

Some interviews will last five minutes, some will last thirty minutes—it all depends on how long the casting person feels he or she needs to get a good idea of who you are and what your *Made* episode could entail. The interviews are very casual: You'll simply talk about your life and what you'd want to change if you could. You should, however, have an idea of how you'd like to be "made" before you sit down in front of the camera—unless you want the casting person to invent a show for you. Aside from that, your best strategy is simply to be yourself and keep the conversation engaging.

Video Application

Most applicants will apply via mail with a video application. If you're between the ages of fifteen and twenty-one, plunk yourself down in front of a video camera and explain who you are, how you'd like to be "made," and why you should be chosen to appear on the show. Your tape should be no longer than five minutes and should give the casting team a good idea of who you are and what your life is like. Explain to your viewers at MTV what help you would like from them: What type of coach would you need? At what types of facilities would you need to train? What kind of schedule would you need to follow? If you're a high school student, it's not a bad idea to take your video camera to school, which will provide the casting team with a taste of what your life is like.

SEND YOUR TAPE TO:

★★★★★★★★★★★★★★★★★★★★★★★

Mail your video (make sure it's either VHS or mini-DV format) and completed application, along with a recent 3x5-or-larger photo of yourself, to:

★★★★★★★★★★★★★★★★★★★★★★★

Made Casting
MTV
770 Broadway
2nd Floor, Suite 238
New York, NY 10003

★★★★★★★★★★★★★★★★★★★★★★★

Remember: The main goal of your tape is to communicate who you are, and how and why you'd like to be "made." You should highlight what's lacking in your life and show how achieving your *Made* goal would dramatically improve your life. Since your friends and family will be involved in your *Made* episode, be sure to talk about how achieving your *Made* goal would affect them: Would they think it was silly? Would they make fun of you? Would they be proud?

WHAT THEY'RE LOOKING FOR

The casting person to whom I spoke put it like this: "There's no real trick to getting on *Made*. It has to be someone who is themselves. Anyone who is savvy enough to figure out how to get on *Made* shouldn't need to be on *Made* in the first place. You can tell if a person really needs help, and we're looking for people who need our help."

If you've watched the show before, you've probably noticed that the people cast on *Made* seem very sincere and "real." This is something that can't be faked—at least not by fifteen-year-olds. The people who get cast on *Made* really do want to change their lives and do something they've always dreamed of doing but have never had the courage to try. You can't smooth-talk your way onto this show.

There are, however, certain traits the casting team looks for in a candidate, and if you think you fit the bill, you should definitely apply. The producers like people with goals that seem easily attainable for the average person, but for one reason or another seem very out-of-reach for that individual. For example, let's say you're the class nerd who has always wanted to be a snowboarder. Okay, no big deal, right? All you have to do is hit the mountain and take a few lessons. But what if you were afraid of heights? Makes it kind of hard to ride that chairlift to the top of the mountain, doesn't it? It's this type of obstacle that *Made*'s casting people love: the girl with the speech impediment who wants to sing, the 125-pound kid who wants to play football, the most popular girly-girl in school who wants to become a boxer. These are the kinds of people who get *Made*.

As one casting person at *Made* puts it, it's all about the "no way!" factor. The casting team wants to see someone, hear what they want to be "made" into, and think to themselves, "no way could that person do that!" If your story can elicit a "no way!" response, you'll be in a much better position to get cast on the show.

As a side note, sometimes the producers themselves come up with the *Made* stories and then go out searching for the right people about whom to tell those stories. In fact, don't be surprised if one of the producers asks you to modify your proposed *Made* story a bit. For example, one high school student who applied for *Made* said he wanted to be "made" into a Samurai. However, since MTV isn't exactly in the business of putting swords into the hands of minors, the producers instead suggested that he learn karate. So if you're willing, don't be surprised if the producers ask you to tweak your story a bit for the sake of making better television.

The moral of the story is this: In order to get *Made*, be yourself—and let them know how sincere you are about wanting to try something new in your life.

It's a lot of information to fit into five minutes worth of videotape, so be concise and get straight to the point.

Once your five-minute video is done, download the show's application from the "Casting Call" section of MTV.com. The application, which needs to be signed by a parent or legal guardian if you're under the age of eighteen, basically asks you to answer the same questions you answered in your video application—only now the casting team wants to see it written down in your own words.

Round Two and Beyond

Because most fifteen-year-olds have the attention spans of gnats, *Made* chooses its casts and goes into production fairly soon after reviewing video applications or holding open calls. In making their decision, the producers and executives at MTV will review your package with a fine-tooth comb to determine what sort of episode they could create from your story. MTV really likes to have control over what type of person and image it allows on the air, so everyone at MTV, from the casting associate to the vice president of programming, will have to give your story the green light in order for the production company to dedicate an entire episode to you.

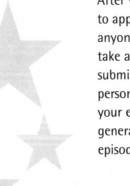

After you submit your application, and even if you are selected to appear on the show, you probably won't see or hear from anyone at MTV until they start filming your episode. It may take anywhere from six weeks to three months after the submission of your application for the show to contact you personally, but if MTV is interested in you, it will be planning your episode, talking with your friends and family, and generally conspiring behind your back to ensure that your episode comes as a complete surprise to you. Not many people make it to this stage, somewhere in the range of twenty-five or thirty people per season.

Did You Know?

My all time favorite episode of *Made* centered on a homely girl named Andi who wanted to be homecoming queen. But wait, there's more. As homecoming queen she wanted to wear a homemade prom dress made from nothing but duct tape. You heard me: duct tape.

PIMP MY RIDE

STAT SHEET

PREMISE:
Rapper Xzibit takes busted-up cars and "pimps" them into shiny, like-new vehicular masterpieces that better suit their young, hip owners.

HOST:
Xzibit

NETWORK:
MTV

YEARS RUNNING:
First aired in March 2004

CONTACT:
MTV–Phone: (310) 907-2688
Web: *www.mtv.com*
E-mail: pmrcasting@mtvstaff.com (Southern California)
pmrusa@mtvstaff.com (everywhere else)

CREATORS:
Rick Hurvitz, Bruce Beresford-Redman

EXECUTIVE PRODUCER:
Bruce Beresford-Redman

CONTESTANT AGE RANGE:
18–22

NUMBER OF APPLICANTS PER SEASON:
5,000

NUMBER OF CONTESTANTS CHOSEN:
One person and one car per episode, 5–15 episodes per season

There once was a time when asking a person if you could "pimp his ride" would have caused that person to furrow his brow and look at you as if you were insane, while perplexing images of men in fur coats and deviant acts danced in his head. But that time has come and gone. Today, to offer a young man or woman a chance to have his or her "ride pimped" generally elicits the immediate response "Fo' shizzle!" as the lucky winner hops up and down, smiling and whooping with glee. These are strange times we live in.

On *Pimp My Ride*, hip-hop superstar and well-meaning rapper Xzibit takes your dowdy, bedraggled vehicle and, like the pumpkin in *Cinderella*, transforms it into a vehicular masterpiece. But enough about that. . . you just want to know how to get X-to-the-Z to show up at your crib, don't you? Let's pimp some rides here, people!

The Audition Process

As of the writing of this book, MTV is casting for *Pimp My Ride* only in the Southern California area. The casting director explained to me that the network is hoping to start casting nationwide soon, but that the holdup is a matter of logistics: Getting your junked-up car all the way out to Los Angeles, or getting West Coast Customs (the company that does the "ride pimping") to your neck of the woods is no small feat. It looks like MTV will eventually get it figured out, however, so you non-Californians should not feel discouraged about applying. After all, the more you people from all over the country apply, the more reasons MTV will have to get out of California and film you.

When applying to any MTV show, first visit *www.MTV.com* and click on "Shows," then "Casting Calls." This is where the network lists every show that is in the process of casting. If *Pimp My Ride* is casting, you can find out here. The Web site should also provide you with an up-to-date hotline number for applying to the show.

First things first: Call the hotline. You'll hear a message instructing you to send MTV an E-mail. Note that although you could skip the hotline step and simply send in an E-mail, it's best to make sure that no information has changed before you go to the trouble of applying.

There are certain criteria you and your car must meet in order to be eligible for *Pimp My Ride*. The rules are as follows

★ You must be between eighteen and twenty-two years old.

★ Your car must be in working condition. If you need a tow truck to get around in your car, *Pimp My Ride* is not for you.

★ The deed for the car must be in *your* name—*not* your parents' name.

★ The car must be insured, and you must have proof of this insurance.

If you still fit the bill, it's time to put your E-mail together. Here's what the E-mail should include:

- Your name, age, and the city you're from

- Year and make of your car

- One picture of yourself in front of your car and a few pictures of your car by itself, with interior and exterior shots

- Your story, i.e., what makes you worthy of having your ride pimped (see the "What They're Looking For" section of this chapter for more information on how to craft your story)

If you live in Southern California, send your E-mail to pmrcasting@mtvstaff.com.
If you live anywhere else, send your E-mail to pmrusa@mtvstaff.com.

Round Two and Beyond

If the MTV casting team is interested in you, your car, and your story, they'll call you in for an audition at the MTV offices in Los Angeles. You'll need to bring your car with you to the audition, so, once again, if you have to tow your car to the MTV offices, you're wasting your time and money.

Once at MTV, you'll fill out a short questionnaire so the casting team can gather more information about your background, education, and personality. Then they'll take you outside and film a quick interview in which you stand in front of your car and explain why your ride should be pimped. They'll ask you questions like: "What's the most embarrassing thing that ever happened to you because of your car?"; "How do your friends and family feel about your car?"; and "What's it like to pick up a date in your car?" Basically, the casting team wants to form an idea about the story they could build around you and your car. (More on that later.) After your interview, they'll ask you to drive your hunk of junk off their lot and wait six to eight weeks to hear from them.

If you do get a call, it will be a producer letting you know that you're a finalist. At that point, you'll be asked to come back to the MTV offices with your car so the casting team can get to know even more about you. This time, they'll want to know everything about your friends and family and how to get them involved in the show. For the casting team, the goal of this meeting is to develop the idea for a potential episode they can pitch to MTV executives.

MTV is one of the few networks at which the head honchos like to personally green-light each person who gets cast on its shows. Once you are a finalist, your application will make it all the way to the desks of MTV's vice president and president of Production. This exhaustive process is all part of MTV's attempt to keep the channel hip, fresh, and cutting-edge at all times. If the boys in the corner office like you, the producers will have their blessing to pimp your ride.

Finally, the producers will call to inform you that you are one of three finalists. Each finalist will be instructed to be at his or her house, with his or her car in the driveway, on a certain date and at a certain time. The producers will tell you that a camera crew will arrive at each of the three finalists' houses, but that only one camera crew will have Xzibit with it, and only one person will get his or her ride pimped.

In all actuality, there aren't two other finalists waiting for camera crews to show up at their houses; they just tell you this so you look surprised and excited when Xzibit shows up on your doorstep. But don't tell them I told you this, and please try to act surprised—after all, MTV is about to spend $30,000 pimping your ride. Get amped!

What They're Looking For In You

The type of story *Pimp My Ride* likes to tell is that of the average down-and-out recent college grad trying to find his or her way in the world—a person for whom the only thing holding him or her back from taking that next step is the monstrosity of a car in which he or she is forced to drive around.

An ideal story, featured on an early episode of *Pimp My Ride*, was that of a first-year law student at USC who was embarrassed to show up to job interviews, because every time she got out of her junky car she had pieces of the seat and ceiling plastered all over her clothing. Once her car was "pimped," she was able to show up at her interviews cleanly and proudly—with her clothes fully steamed and pressed by the steamer that was installed in her trunk by the good people at West Coast Customs. Now the car fits her personality and, instead of impeding her progress, is helping her move ahead in life.

The key to getting cast on *Pimp My Ride* is this: You have to love your car, and not want to get rid of it, but it has to be holding you back because it's so messed up. If only your car better matched your personality, then, and only then, could you move on with your life in confidence and style. If you can build your story around that premise, you'll be golden.

Did You Know?

Getting your ride pimped ain't cheap. The average custom job done by West Coast Customs (the company that does all the pimping for *Pimp My Ride*) will set one back a cool thirty grand. Or you could just buy one of their pre-pimped cars, which sell online or at their garage in Los Angeles: They start at around ninety thousand smackeroos.

WHAT THEY'RE LOOKING FOR IN YOUR CAR

Pimp My Ride gets a lot of people who show up for interviews driving a Honda with a ripped seat and broken radio. These people obviously don't understand the concept of the show. The casting team is *not* looking for cars in semi-mint condition; they're looking for the ugliest cars in the world. The worse your car looks, the better it's going to look on the show. Your car has to be the kind of car that elicits screams from children when you drive down the street—which brings me to another important point, which is that your car has to be *able* to drive down the street.

That's right: All cars must be drivable. Why, you ask? Because the "pimping" done at West Coast Customs is purely cosmetic. The show's casting people told me that West Coast Customs will perform a small amount of engine work on your car if it needs it—an oil change or fan belt replacement, for example—but that's about it. This is *not* a chance for you to get your car repaired; it's a chance for you to get your car "pimped." After all, the show isn't called *Repair My Car.* Why? Because *that* show would be boring.

Also, you won't see many cars from the 1950s or 1960s on the show, because vintage cars are almost too difficult to "pimp." The parts are hard to find and replace, and the mechanisms on some convertibles tend to be rusted beyond repair.

The bottom line is this: *Pimp My Ride* is looking for a car that can get you from point A to point B, that's less than thirty years old, and that looks a lot worse than it drives.

QUEER EYE FOR THE STRAIGHT GUY
AND
QUEER EYE FOR THE STRAIGHT GIRL

Don't tell me you've never watched *Queer Eye* and thought to yourself "Wow, those shower curtain rings really *did* make that bathroom!" I'm a straight guy, but I swear my life has become a little more stylish since this uber-hip makeover show went on the air.

Things I've learned from watching *Queer Eye*: always apply hair products starting from the back; never leave the house wearing a tucked-in shirt with no belt; and add a dash of color to a wall to bring any room to life. I swear I'm still straight though.

Now, let's get our gay on!

STAT SHEET

PREMISE:

Guy—Five gay men, commonly known as the "Fab Five," take straight men with no sense of style and turn them into chic metrosexuals.

Girl—Four gay men and one lesbian remake, remodel, and rejuvenate frumpy young lasses.

HOSTS:

Guy—Ted Allan (Food & Wine Connoisseur), Kyan Douglas (Grooming Guru), Thom Filicia (Design Doctor), Carson Kressley (Fashion Savant), Jai Rodriguez (Culture Vulture)

Girl—Robbie Laughlin (The Look), Danny Teeson (The Life), Damon Pease (The Locale), Honey Labrador (The Lady)

NETWORK:
Bravo

YEARS RUNNING:
Guy—First aired in July 2003; *Girl*—first aired in 2004

CONTACT:
Web: *www.bravotv.com*

PRODUCTION COMPANY:
Scout Productions

CREATOR:
David Collins

EXECUTIVE PRODUCERS:
Dorothy Aufiero (*Guy*), David Collins (*Girl*)

CONTESTANT AGE RANGE:
18 and up

NUMBER OF APPLICANTS PER SEASON:
10,000

NUMBER OF CONTESTANTS CHOSEN:
One per episode, 10–25 episodes per season

The Audition Process

As of the writing of this book, *Queer Eye* casts only people who live in either the New York City or Los Angeles metropolitan areas. Hopefully the show will start looking for guys and gals in other areas, but for now, only the coastal big-city folk stand a chance.

Though *Queer Eye* occasionally holds open calls in New York and Los Angeles, the best way onto the show is also the easiest: through the Web site. Simply visit *www.bravotv.com* and select either *Queer Eye* show from the network's programming list. If the show is casting, you'll see a button on the *Queer Eye* page that reads "Be on the Show." Click that button, and away you go.

Online Application

Since *Queer Eye* is a very image-conscious show, you'll first be required to upload a recent picture of yourself. Simply find your favorite photo of yourself on your computer (or, if you're a caveman, scan an actual printed photo), and upload the image onto the show's Web site. It doesn't matter what size the picture is, or even what you're doing in the picture, although the casting team does recommend a close-up shot. Also, if you're sending in a group photo, make sure you indicate which of the people in the photo is you.

The next step is to fill out a short online application with your most basic personal information and a simple description of your home or apartment. The application also includes three essay questions, which focus on why you want to be on *Queer Eye*, what the Fab Five could do for you, and what goals you hope to accomplish by appearing on the show.

Once you've completed your application, simply click "Send in Your Application!" and you'll have done just that. You're on your way!

Round Two and Beyond

It's hard to say how many people make it to the second round of casting, considering the quality of applicants is inconsistent, but from what I gather, somewhere around a quarter of all the people who apply get at least one follow-up phone call. If the casting directors like your picture and think your story has potential, they'll call you on the phone for a brief chat—just to make sure you're not a total psycho—and then invite you to the studio for a filmed interview. Interviews last around thirty minutes and are conversational and laid-back. If the interview goes well, the casting team will then send a crew out to film your house.

They'll then pitch your edited tape to the *Queer Eye* producers and Bravo network executives. If everyone's in agreement that watching you get a makeover would make for a great hour of television, well, then you're just the luckiest straight man or woman on Gay Street, aren't you?

Did You Know?

Before he was known for putting straight men into pleated pants, fashion aficianado Carson Kressley spent his time competing as a ranked equestrian. Although he competes only for fun nowadays, Carson still loves to dote on his horse named George, whom he keeps in a stable in Union, Kentucky.

WHAT THEY'RE LOOKING FOR

Well, for starters, you've got to be straight (though I think it would be a crime if someone didn't also make *Queer Eye for the Queer Girl* someday).

Aside from being straight, you and your apartment have got to be a mess—and not the type of mess you can fake ten minutes before the camera crews show up at your door by mussing your hair and throwing a pizza box on the floor. Typical Fab Five makeover recipients are people (and apartments) whose dowdy looks have been years—nay, decades—in the making. If even one person (aside from your roommate) can visit your apartment without commenting on how horrible it looks, then don't bother applying. If you open a fashion magazine and see people who look like you, dress like you, or have their hair styled like you, don't bother applying.

Now, this isn't to say that the casting team considers only unattractive applicants with depressing apartments—far from it. What they're looking for is attractive people with nice apartments who have simply let things go for a bit too long. Keep in mind that the goal of your makeover is to make people say "Wow, that person *was* attractive and his (or her) apartment *was* really nice—all he (or she) needed was a little tszujing!" (pronounced "szhu-shzing" and is a fancy way of saying "finesse").

As important as your look, however, is your story. *Queer Eye* casts for people who are on the verge of major events in their lives. Ever notice how almost every *Queer Eye* episode ends with either a big party, or a big dinner, or a big date? This is not just because gays like to celebrate; it's because Bravo likes to tell a good yarn. The network wants to build a story around you—one that either culminates in an event you've been waiting for your whole life, or that forces you to overcome an obstacle that's been holding you back for a long time. Whether you're about to propose to your longtime girlfriend or you haven't been on a date in six years, you're going to have to figure out what your big event is going to be and then sell it to the casting team as part of your package (calm down, boys).

The bottom line: If you've got a frumpy look, an apartment that time forgot, and a life-changing event on your horizon, then you're an ideal candidate for *Queer Eye*. Do it to it.

RENOVATE MY FAMILY

Renovate My Family, FOX's answer to *Extreme Makeover: Home Edition,* gives down-on-their-luck families a second chance by remodeling their homes and helping them reshape their lives.

The Audition Process

Because they are both produced by Rocket Science Productions, *Renovate My Family* and *Trading Spouses* use identical casting processes. In fact, both shows usually cast at the same time. Visit the FOX Web site (*www.fox.com*) for open-call information or to apply online. Note that there are separate mailing addresses for applications from Southern California.

STAT SHEET

PREMISE:
Entire families receive life-altering,
tear-jerking makeovers.

HOST:
Jay McGraw

NETWORK:
FOX

YEARS RUNNING:
Season 1 first aired in 2004.

CONTACT:
Rocket Science—Phone: (323) 802-0500
Web: *www.fox.com/renovatemyfamily*

PRODUCTION COMPANY:
Rocket Science

EXECUTIVE PRODUCERS:
Chris Cowan, Jean-Michel Michenaud, Ray Guiliani

CONTESTANT AGE RANGE:
All ages

NUMBER OF APPLICANTS PER SEASON:
5,000 families

NUMBER OF CONTESTANTS CHOSEN:
One family per show (number of family
members varies), ten episodes per season.

WHAT THEY'RE LOOKING FOR

A useful rule of thumb is this: The more dire your family's situation, the more dramatic your renovation will be, and the better television viewing it will make—thus, the more likely you are to get cast on *Renovate My Family*.

While the show doesn't cast *only* families with tragic sob stories, those families with less emotionally charged stories usually have some other sort of dramatic "hook." An episode during Season One, for example, featured a "Goth" family whose daughter wanted them to be made over into a more "normal" family. What made this episode more than just a modern-day Munsters makeover, however, was that the non-Goth daughter slept on the couch in the living room and felt totally ostracized from her family. Though the episode was light and fun, it was also heartfelt and emotional. The lesson here is that if you're going to go for the "wacky" angle in your application, you're going to need to find an equivalent emotional "hook" around which the producers can build an episode.

As a side note, the show's casting director told me that the one thing that never ceases to amaze her is the number of applicants who have really, really normal families, but who nonetheless see themselves as completely "crazy." Note to families: The mere fact that you don't have a Jacuzzi in your living room doesn't mean your family is falling apart.

Did You Know?

Host Jay McGraw is the son of self-help evangelist and Oprah protégé Dr. Phil. Before *Renovate My Family*, Jay was known for authoring a series of self-help books on bridging parent-teenager relations. He also has written his own teen weight loss manual, *The Ultimate Weight Solution for Teens.* Now all he needs is an M.D. Unfortunately, I think the name "Dr. J" is already taken.

THE SWAN

STAT SHEET

PREMISE:
In each episode, filmed over a three-month period, two women receive a "total life makeover." A panel of judges then decides who has undergone the greater transformation—from ugly duckling to The Swan. At the end of the season, the episode winners participate in a pageant, the winner of which is crowned "The Ultimate Swan."

HOST:
Amanda Byram

NETWORK:
FOX

YEARS RUNNING:
Season 1 first aired in April of 2004.

CONTACT:
FOX—Phone: (800) 535-7936   Web: *www.fox.com/swan*

PRODUCTION COMPANY:
FremantleMedia and GALAN Entertainment

CREATOR:
Nely Galan

EXECUTIVE PRODUCERS:
Arthur Smith, Nely Galan

CO-EXECUTIVE PRODUCER:
Kent Weed

CONTESTANT AGE RANGE:
21–45

NUMBER OF APPLICANTS PER SEASON:
10,000

NUMBER OF CONTESTANTS CHOSEN:
Two per episode, ten episodes per season

"It's kind of heartbreaking to cast *The Swan*," one of the show's casting directors told me. Having to pick through thousands of applications telling tragic stories, and then pick the few applicants who seem most deserving of change, is not an enviable task.

For the first season of *The Swan*, the show's directors faced a serious casting dilemma: How do you advertise for unattractive people with heartbreaking life stories? I mean, who would come to a casting call like that? So instead of waiting for women to come to them, the casting department set out to find the women themselves—traveling all over the country to battered women's shelters, plastic-surgery clinics, and self-help groups, searching high and low for women who fit *The Swan*'s bill (no pun intended).

They succeeded.

The Audition Process

In its first season, the show was an instant hit. As a result, subsequent seasons have been much easier to cast, and the casting team now employs a more traditional reality-TV casting process.

If you think you're a perfect contestant for *The Swan*, you have two application paths to chose from: an open casting call or a video application. Here's how they both work:

Open Casting Calls

Check FOX's Web site (*www.fox.com*) to find out about open casting calls near you. If there's no casting information available online, the show is most likely off-season, which means that it's not casting right now, and producers are unsure when the next casting cycle will begin. If the show is currently casting, the Web site will provide up-to-date information on the dates and locations of casting calls. FOX also likes to advertise open calls on its local affiliate stations during prime time, on local radio morning shows, or on fliers handed out at popular locations such as shopping centers or fairs.

The Swan's open casting calls use the "group interview" method, in which you and nine other people are interviewed together during a five- to ten-minute period. In roundtable fashion, each person will be asked to talk a little bit about herself, and to give a few reasons why she thinks she'd make a good contestant on *The Swan*.

Remember, keep it short. Each person only gets a minute or two to speak, so make sure you get through everything you want to say—you don't want to get cut off mid-sentence with a curt "I'm sorry, but we have a lot of people to get through today and we need to let everyone speak." That's never a good casting call moment, so be brief. Also, it doesn't hurt to practice what you're going to say before going in.

Just tell your story, be as honest as you can, let your personality shine through as much as possible, and make sure the casting team knows how badly you want to be on the show. Spend the entire minute detailing your troubled past, highlight the worst events from your life (as long as they are somehow connected to your physical appearance or mental outlook), and try to end it on a mildly positive note: something along the lines of "but now I'm here because I feel only *The Swan* can help me, and I'm ready to change my life." Remember: They're going to be spending more than a hundred thousand dollars on you if you're chosen to receive a "total life makeover," so do your best to convince them that you need the makeover more than anyone else in the room.

In addition to participating in the group interview, expect to fill out a short application consisting of general personal information and a few short-answer questions about your life, your hardships, and your hopes for the future.

If the casting team liked what you had to say during the group interview, you'll be stopped on your way out and asked to complete a long application, which will contain a series of longer questions about your past, your hardships, and your goals and aspirations. Once that's filled out, there's nothing left to do but hope you get a phone call during the next few days from someone in the casting department.

Video Application

Unlike *Survivor*, *American Idol*, and *The Real World*, which cast at least once a year and rarely change their casting procedures, shows like *The Swan* are a bit unpredictable, and don't always cast during the same period each year. Therefore, make sure the show is casting before you send in your video application, or else your tape may never make it into the right hands.

Your video application should present the same information you would present if you attended an open call. The tape should be no more than three minutes long, and should feature you sitting in front of the camera, shot from the shoulders up, talking briefly about yourself and explaining why you should be chosen as a contestant on *The Swan*. Be sure not to exceed the three-minute mark by even a second; in fact, I recommend shooting for about two and a half minutes. Treat the video camera exactly as you would an interviewer at the open call: Simply tell your story, let the casting team get a good look at you, and plead your case.

When your videotape is completed (either in VHS or mini-DV format), go online and download the show's short application, which is self-explanatory and simply asks for some general personal information and a few short answers to questions about your life.

Round Two and Beyond

If you get a phone call after attending an open call or submitting a video application, you'll be asked to fill out a longer application and come to the closest "numbered city" for a second interview. The "numbered cities" are essentially the six biggest cities in the country, divided into zones, with each zone relegated to a different casting director. In this round of the audition process, you'll be expected to cover your own costs for travel and accommodations.

Expect a thirty-minute, in-person, taped interview in which you'll face questions similar to those in the long application you filled out; in fact, be prepared to speak about everything and anything you wrote on that application.

If the casting director is pleased with your long interview, you'll be flown out to Los Angeles and put up in a hotel—all on the show's dime—while the casting team interviews you ad nauseum for an entire weekend. If they—meaning the producers and a few FOX network executives—think you're right for the show, then you'll become one of twenty finalists who will appear on *The Swan*, and your makeover will be on its way.

SEND YOUR TAPE AND APPLICATION TO:

★★★★★★★★★★★★★★★★★★★★★★★

The Swan Casting Department
2554 Lincoln Blvd
PMB #1013
Venice, CA 90291

★★★★★★★★★★★★★★★★★★★★★★★

WHAT THEY'RE LOOKING FOR

First off, they're not looking for men. Let's just get that out of the way. The casting people told me they receive lots of applications from men, so let's do them all a favor and save them a trip to the bin to throw away your tape. Maybe one day they'll do version of *The Swan* for men called *Ugly Duckling* or something like that (wait. . . someone already made a show called *Ugly Duckling*), but for now *The Swan* is women only. Sorry, fellas!

A casting director summed it up best when she told me, "We want somebody who's driven, who has had a hard life and is down on themselves, but not to the point where they're not willing to do anything about it." *The Swan* is designed to be a tearjerker. It's what would have been referred to in old television talk as a "weepie." So the casting team wants to find people with the most extreme tales of woe, who have suffered through so much ridicule and insecurity based on their looks that their quality of life has been severely affected.

But they also want people who, through all of that pain and suffering, still hold onto hope that one day things will be better. Another casting director told me, "There's some people who are in a situation and they're so down on themselves and so negative that we fear they don't have the drive to change themselves—that they won't commit to anything." These are the people who don't make it onto *The Swan*. You've got to be enthusiastic and determined to change.

In many cases, it just comes down to the emotional resonance of your hard-luck story. This is going to sound horrible, but most people who feel they're unattractive or who have battled with insecurity have at least one or two good horror stories from their childhood. That doesn't make them interesting enough for *The Swan*. At *The Swan*, they're looking for horror stories to end all horror stories.

Just to give you an example of what they're looking for, one woman featured in the show's first season had a condition called "web neck": an excess of skin on her neck that gave her an unnatural appearance. When she was a child, other children used to spit on her and call her names. As if that wasn't bad enough, once she was an adult, even her own daughter tormented her and called her "cobra." Her own daughter! Everyone's got a few bad stories in his or her past, but I dare you to compete with the woman who gets called "cobra" by her own daughter. So, not to dissuade you from applying, but just be aware that in order to qualify for an extreme makeover (wait. . . wrong show), you've got to have an extreme sob story.

Aside from the sob story, *The Swan* likes to emphasize the "second-chance" factor of each contestant. Not only is *The Swan* concerned with re-vamping someone's exterior, it also wants to help facilitate a mental and emotional rejuvenation. Make sure the casting department knows you're as open to a new attitude as you are to a new body.

Bottom line is to just be yourself, show them you've got stoic determination, and don't be afraid to squeeze out a few tears in your interview—whatever it takes to get that total life makeover! Oh boy. . . I feel dirty now.

If you make it on the show, be prepared to be away from your family, your job, and your friends for three entire months. When they watch the show, some people don't realize how extensive a commitment is involved for the contestants—so before you get to this point in the audition process, make sure you understand what will be expected of you if you're cast.

Did You Know?

The Dublin-born host of *The Swan*, Amanda Byram, was also the host of the reality TV show *Paradise Hotel*, known as one of the sleaziest reality shows of all time. The premise was simple: lots of single men and women were stuck together in "paradise," and basically, if they didn't hook up with someone, get naked, or do something crazy, they got eliminated at the end of the week and replaced by people who answered a few trivia questions correctly on the show's Web site. Paradise, indeed.

Interview
Nely Galan, Creator of *The Swan*

MR: Tell me how *The Swan* came to be.

NG: It came very much from my own life, my own ideas. I had a baby, so I was a single mom, and I just thought, "What would I want right now if I could have anything in the world?" And I thought I'd want to go away to a spa, get a nutritionist, get a workout coach, get a boob lift—because I had just breast-fed a baby—and I thought, "My god, that's a TV show." And like all producers do, you come up with an idea, it settles in your brain, some of them you forget about, and some of them keep coming back. What happened with me was, I was reading my kid's storybook of Hans Christian Andersen's stories, and I got to "The Ugly Duckling," and when I saw the words "the swan," I was like, "Oh my god, this is a hit show." I knew.

MR: Did you know your role going in? Did you always want to be the life coach?

NG: No, no, no. In fact, I wasn't supposed to be the life coach. I always knew there should be a life coach in the show, because I've hired life coaches and they've really been good for me. They've helped me with work and different things in my life. The role of a life coach is to be tough on you, and we were looking at different life coaches, and the people at FOX looked at me and said, "You should do it; you're tougher than everyone else." And that's how it came to be. It was not initially planned that I'd do it.

MR: What makes a great *Swan* contestant?

NG: Someone who is really at a crossroads in their life. To me, the show is about death and resurrection. Things happen to us in our lives that make us go, "Life isn't what we thought it was going to be." And you think, "I'm never going to be happy again." And the truth is that you can be happy again—in fact, you can be happier than you think. For me, the perfect candidate is someone who feels that way, someone in a "victim" place, because for me the show is about taking someone's victimization and turning it around for them.

MR: What do you think has made *The Swan* so popular?

NG: You have to remember I'm a Latin girl from Latin America, so I have a very different perspective on the world than most people. When I go to visit my relatives in Cuba, I realize that the concerns of people in the Third World are much more about survival. For good or for bad, we have the privilege in the United States to really make the most of ourselves because we're not dealing with survival issues. We're a society that is open to therapy. I mean, look how many self-help gurus we have, whereas in other countries they don't. I think we live in a time when we have, as I said, the privilege to really work on ourselves. I think it's very accessible and very appealing to know that you can change your life. It's part of the American dream. I mean, people come here to change their economic status, why not change their status based on how you look or how you feel about yourself?

I find it interesting, because people who are most critical of the show are men, and yet no one would ever question a man for changing his status in the world or dating some young chick because he makes a lot of money. What people don't realize is, beauty and confidence for women is akin to money and power for men. I find it very interesting. It's all a big sociology class to me.

MR: What do you think the difference is between reality-TV programming for English-speaking audiences and Spanish-speaking audiences?

NG: Very different. I feel I'm a niche person. My niche used to be just the Latin market. I think my mentors taught me to do work from what I know, and that way I'll always stand out, because it's what I really know and no one else can do it better than me. When I was in the Latin market, for me it was about telling stories about Latinos in the U.S., and I felt very comfortable telling those stories. In the English-speaking market, I feel I've found a new niche, which is the woman niche. I know what it is to be a woman. And a woman in a post-feminist time, with all the tug-of-war that we have between being women and taking care of others and yet being powerhouses. I think that's my voice in the Anglo-market. What I try and do is find the common denominator with women. My views on being a minority woman give me an advantage, because I'm able to see to that section of the audience in a way that a male Reality producer can't.

MR: What do you think draws people to reality TV?

NG: Human beings ultimately want to watch themselves, and reality TV has really shown people that reality is stranger than fiction. Ultimately, the stars of reality TV are real people. I find it fascinating, because we spend so many years idolizing celebrities, and now real people get a shot at it, and of course they love it.

When I watch reality shows, I really can detach myself from being a producer. I know when a reality show is a hit, because I'm jealous that I'm not on the show. When I first saw *The Bachelorette,* I was jealous I wasn't on the show. I was jealous that I wasn't on *Survivor.* I think that must be the way the audience feels. I'd love to take a few months and go hang out with Donald Trump and see what he lives like. It's an adventure. Why wouldn't I want to do that?

MR: Aside from the ones you work on, what's your favorite reality TV show?

NG: I'm a reality-TV fanatic. I certainly love *The Bachelor* series. I love anything Mark Burnett does—I'm a big fan of his. I think the thought process of Reality producers is fascinating. It's about finding an idea that gets people to do something they'd never think about doing. I always loved *Trading Spaces.* I love *Project Runway.* I love all the dating ones. I loved Branson's show; the first episode was out of the park. I loved *My Big Fat Obnoxious Fiancé,* and I loved the boxing show on FOX. I'm a boxing fanatic. I just thought the show was so well put together; it was eye candy. I love reality shows that move me. Oh wait—I remember what my favorite reality show is now: *Nanny 911!* I cry every fricking week. That's one show I'm always jealous I'm not on. I need *Nanny 911.* Being on a reality show is like hitting the lottery for a lot of these people. I want to be on a reality show. You get pampered, treated like kings; it's like an adventure vacation.

MR: Do you have a favorite *Swan* episode?

NG: My favorite personal moment was with Delisa (the girl who won the second season of *The Swan*), because her husband served her with divorce papers while she was on the show. I went to see her and I completely forgot I was a life coach or a producer, and we both started crying hysterically because we all know what it's like to break up with someone. She was like a little animal that was in pain. I couldn't help it; I was hysterical with her. It was the most real moment of the whole experience.

MR: What do you think is next for reality TV?

NG: I don't think reality TV is going anywhere. The stakes are higher though. There aren't many Reality producers. Everybody used to think it was low-class to do Reality, that the place to go was to do fiction, so a lot of these big producers didn't focus on Reality, so there were only a few big producers in the game. Now every Tom, Dick, and Harry wants to produce Reality. So now the stakes are higher. Shows have to be more creative.

To produce Reality is the most fun thing for a producer—it's a producer's medium. When you go to produce fiction, the writers take over and the producers are kind of cast aside. In reality TV, you come up with the idea, you are the writer of the idea, you mold it, and you're the star of the show. It's your baby. It's a very pleasant work experience. It's very action-packed; it's a lot of fun for a type A personality. Real things happen that can change the course of the show midway, so it keeps you on your toes. Doing reality shows is the most fun I've ever had in my life.

MR: What's next for Nely Galan and Galan Entertainment?

NG: I'm going to continue to have one foot in the Hispanic market and one foot in my new niche, which is chick shows. I'm doing three projects simultaneously. One is called *Miss Mogul* for Lifetime, and then two shows for Telemundo, one called *Prince Charming* and the other called *Green Card*.

PART III

Adventure/Competition Shows

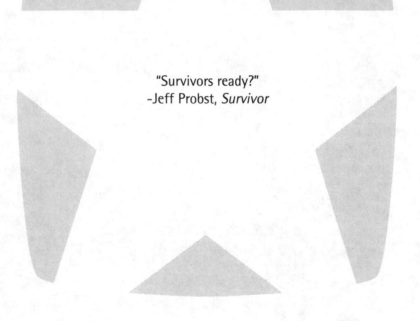

"Survivors ready?"
-Jeff Probst, *Survivor*

Far and away the most popular form of reality TV, adventure/competition shows rip game shows out of the television studio and toss them into the "real world." And because they're game shows, adventure/competition shows can mean big bucks for the winners.

THE AMAZING RACE

STAT SHEET

PREMISE:
Teams of two race around the world, completing various tasks along the way. The first team to reach the finish line wins a million bucks.

HOST:
Phil Keoghan

NETWORK:
CBS

YEARS RUNNING:
Season 1 first aired in September of 2001.

CONTACT:
CBS—Phone: (323) 575-2345
Web: *www.cbs.com*

PRODUCTION COMPANY:
Jerry Bruckheimer Television, Earthview Productions, Worldrace Productions

CREATORS:
Elise Doganieri, Bertram van Munster

EXECUTIVE PRODUCERS:
Jerry Bruckheimer, Bertram van Munster, Jonathan Littman

CONTESTANT AGE RANGE:
21 and up

NUMBER OF APPLICANTS PER SEASON:
20,000

NUMBER OF CONTESTANTS CHOSEN:
So far, either eleven or twelve couples per season

To most, the idea of spending a few weeks traversing four continents, racing to over twenty countries, beating out other couples at extreme stunts, and doing it all with a loved one in tow, would sound completely exhausting. Well, what if the couple who did it the fastest won a million bucks? Sign me up!

So you want to be on *The Amazing Race*? Well, welcome to the big boys. *The Amazing Race* isn't a show that has trouble getting contestants. The producers don't pass out fliers or do any street recruiting—this is Jerry Bruckheimer, people! This producer's a busy man! So let's not waste his time. The competition is fierce, but here's how you're gonna get on the show. Listen close now.

The Audition Process

First, you need to find out if the show is casting. At least one, if not two, seasons of *The Amazing Race* are produced each year, and the casting process takes three months, so there's a large "window" within which the show will accept applications each year. Watch CBS during prime time and visit *www.CBS.com* for the most up-to-date information. You can also download the application, which you'll need later, at *http://www.cbs.com/primetime/amazing_race_application/.* This link is usually functional, even off-season, so if the show isn't casting at the moment you can still use your time wisely by getting the application filled out perfectly.

The application is ten pages long, and both members of the team need to fill it out individually. The questions are fairly straightforward: "Tell us something about yourself," "Tell us something about your teammate," "What's your favorite/least favorite thing about yourself and your teammate?" Pretty basic stuff.

Make sure you complete the entire application, using as many lines as the application provides for your answers. Don't give any one-word answers. Be sure to elaborate, be specific, and write legibly. If you have bad handwriting, find someone with good handwriting to write out your application for you.

Most reality shows stipulate that no one may reapply to the show after previously applying and being rejected—but not so with *The Amazing Race*. As long as you apply with a *new teammate*, you're considered a new applicant. So if one combination doesn't work, find a new buddy and let the network try the new duo on for size. But keep in mind that, if the casting directors remember your face, they might compare and contrast your old application package with your new one.

Open Calls

Information regarding open calls for *The Amazing Race* can be found on your local CBS affiliates during prime time. Announcements will let you know the time and place of calls and will usually direct you to your local affiliate's Web site to download an application, which, by the way, is the same application you can download directly from the CBS Web site. Complete the short application, grab your buddy, and head down to the open call. While there's no age cutoff for *The Amazing Race*, all applicants must be over the age of twenty-one.

CBS open calls tend to feel more like cattle calls than television auditions. Thousands of people stand in a long line, surrounded by metal gates, waiting for hours on end to be ushered, two by two, in front of a camera. Once in front of the camera, each team has two to three minutes to state its case as to why it would make a great contestant pairing on *The Amazing Race*.

Have your two to three minutes planned out before you arrive, even if that means writing a script and memorizing it beforehand. Unlike the video application, the open call doesn't give you the luxury of second takes—so make sure you and your partner have your routine down pat.

Sometimes open calls feature an entire row of cameras filming multiple people at the same time in "red-carpet" interview fashion. If this is the case, don't let the couple next to you—the one who's jumping up and down and screaming at the camera—distract you. Focus, be yourself, and talk directly to the camera.

If the casting directors like your submission, you won't find out that day, so don't get discouraged on your way home. Your videotape and application will be sent back to the casting department in Los Angeles, and it could take them weeks to get back to you. Be patient!

Video Application

The Amazing Race wants a three-minute video of you *and* your partner together. And remember: All you get is three minutes total. The casting team wants to see the two of you together and relating to one another, so don't film separate ninety-second segments and then edit them into one piece. The casting directors are interested in what you bring to the table as a *team* more than as individuals.

The main question you should answer in your video is, "Why are you perfect for *The Amazing Race*?" Talk about your level of competitiveness, provide a brief history of your relationship, and try to be funny and emotional at the same time. The producers want to see passion. They want to see your personality, so let it shine. But most important, make sure they see chemistry between you and your partner—whether that chemistry takes the form of bickering or laughing. No one wants to watch a show about two people traveling around the world together in silence; they want drama and entertainment. So give it to 'em—all in three minutes. You can do it!

On top of your three-minute video and individual applications, you're going to need the following

★ Proof that you have a valid U.S. passport (or that you have applied for a renewal or issuance), i.e., a photocopy of your passport.

★ A passport-sized photo of each applicant, and one recent photo of the two of you together. If you know the whereabouts of an arcade-style photo booth, that's the perfect place to take this kind of picture!

THROW EVERYTHING INTO AN ENVELOPE AND SEND IT TO:

★★★★★★★★★★★★★★★★★★★★★★

The Amazing Race [City #]
1247 Lincoln Blvd, #60
Santa Monica, CA 90401-1711

★★★★★★★★★★★★★★★★★★★★★★

Be sure to include your city number in the address, so the show will know which area's casting director should receive your package.

From the following list, pick the number that corresponds to the city closest to you. (Both teammates need to pick the same number, so if you live in separate cities, one of you will have to travel farther than the other.)

1. *Los Angeles, CA*
2. *Austin, TX*
3. *Chicago, IL*
4. *New York, NY*
5. *Charlotte, NC*
6. *San Francisco, CA*
7. *Miami, FL*
8. *Tallahassee, FL*
9. *Boston, MA*

Got it all sent? Now you just . . . wait.

Round Two and Beyond

The casting directors will compile the application packages they receive according to area, and from each area they'll pick their favorite teams. These teams will then be contacted and asked to fly to their chosen city for the semifinals. Less than a hundred couples per region make it to this round of the audition process.

Now, keep this in mind: The network does not cover the cost of traveling to the semifinals. They won't pay to fly you to your chosen city, and they won't pay for your hotel room or any other amenities. The cost of attending the semifinals is entirely your responsibility. Consider yourself warned.

At the semifinals, you and your teammate will be interviewed together at length by a casting director. The interview will be in front of a camera and can last anywhere from five minutes to half an hour, depending on how the casting director thinks it's going. Now, a twenty-minute interview doesn't mean they don't like you as much as a team they interviewed for thirty minutes. But if you're done after five minutes, you can bet it didn't go too well.

They're gonna ask you personal questions about your lives, about your relationship with one another, about your fears and dreams; this interview is basically a more in-depth version of your three-minute tape. Be sure to let your personalities shine, and to really let the casting directors get a feel for your relationship. Make sure they know who you're going to be, and what you're going to bring to their show.

Once the semifinal interviews are complete, the casting directors will edit the videos and present their favorites to the show's producers. If the producers like your team, you'll be brought in for the finals. Your trip to the finals—airfare to Los Angeles, your hotel room, and all your meals—will be completely paid for by the network.

The contract you signed when you submitted your application indicates that the finals may last as long as ten days, so be prepared to take some time off from work. At this stage in the casting process, it's interview after interview, and whoever can keep smiling and stay chipper the longest has the best chance at making the cut. This is a true test of your endurance—something you'll have to prove all over again if you actually make it onto the show.

Did You Know?

Season five of *The Amazing Race* featured the first small person to be cast in a major network adventure/competition reality show. Charla, with the help of her sister Mirna, made it halfway around the world and lasted until episode seven before being eliminated. Charla's dwarfism did nothing to impede her ability to race. In fact, she beat out half the playing field before packing her bags and heading home, setting the water mark high as the first small person to take on a major adventure/competition reality show.

WHAT THEY'RE LOOKING FOR

The Amazing Race is all about competition. The producers want people who will fight, fight, fight—people who will do anything to win that money, and who will never give up, no matter how tough things get.

They also want drama. They want relationships that will either fall apart or grow stronger. But they want *something* to happen. If you're an estranged-father-and-son team, they'll want to see the two of you come together. If you're a married couple that bickers, they'll want to see your marriage get into trouble, or grow stronger than it's ever been. Basically, they want a couple who will react in *some* way—for better or for worse—when things get stressful on the road, which they will. When choosing a partner it's important to keep these ideas in mind. Your relationship with your partner has to have some sort of hook that the producers can grab a hold of and weave into a storyline.

How do you react to stress? To fatigue? To physical endurance tests? How does your partner react to these conditions? How do you relate to your partner when he/she is under these conditions? These are the questions you need to have answered before you audition. You've got to know what type of couple you're going to be—what kind of "story arc" you can provide for the show's producers—while at the same time proving that you're entertaining enough to hold an audience's attention for thirteen episodes.

The Amazing Race is about as big as it gets in reality TV, and, in my opinion, it's one of the best shows on the air. It's a wild, exciting ride for the couples who get cast, and a great way to test your relationship with someone you love, whether romantically or platonically.

Good luck, and stay strong!

Interview
Brennen Swain, *The Amazing Race 1*

MR: How did you find out about the audition for *The Amazing Race*?

BS: (laughing) It's always about knowing somebody with these kinds of things. I actually knew one of the girls that was casting. I was on during the first season, so this was at a time when no one knew what [the show] was. She had been casting for *Survivor* and had mentioned to me, "We're casting for this new CBS show, it's teams of two racing around the world. I think you and Rob would make a great team—why don't you submit a tape?" We still had to go through the entire process that everyone else did; that's just how I found out about it.

MR: Break down for me what you did with the tape, what your strategy was.

BS: We were going in as guinea pigs in the first season. We didn't know what the show would be about, other than that it was some kind of race around the world, and we knew there were going to be tasks involved, that sort of thing.

It was your typical three-minute audition tape. We had a minute each where we talked about ourselves. I filmed him, he filmed me. And then in the last minute we kind of bantered back and forth, because we knew it would be important to establish what our relationship was. So we tried to talk about our differences, the tightness of our friendship, and why we thought we'd make good television.

I'm a total extreme-sports athlete—I'm not scared of a whole lot—so I went on this total spiel about how I surfed big waves in Bali and raced cars in Daytona. And looking back on it now I probably wouldn't have said any of that, because they're really looking for the opposite.

MR: Why do you say that?

BS: At least on *The Amazing Race*, and I think it applies to a lot of reality shows as well, there's three ways to get air time. The first one is to screw up, the second one is to be afraid of things, and the third one is to fight, whether it's with teammates or with other people. They want the people that, when they're going to bungee jump, are so afraid that they don't want to do it. So I'm sitting there saying, "Oh, yeah, I'm not afraid of any of that stuff; that kind of stuff is easy." I realize now that probably wasn't the smartest thing to say.

So that's what we did: we talked about what our differences were, what our strengths were. You know, we're both lawyers, so we said "Oh, we know that everyone loves to hate the lawyers, so who knows, maybe we'll turn out to be your villains!"—which we didn't turn out to be. So, we just tried to come up with those things that could be our niche.

MR: And so you sent off the tape. Tell me what happened after that.

BS: The tapes were due on December 15th, and we got a call right before the holidays saying that they wanted us to come in for a half-hour interview. At that point, what they do is, the casting directors fly out, there's nine different cities throughout the country where they audition people. It's up to you to get to that city. Lucky for me, I'm here in L.A.—and L.A. is, of course, one of those cities. We drove down to a hotel in Santa Monica and had a half-hour interview, together.

MR: What did they ask you in the Round Two interview?

BS: They asked us about our relationship, how well we knew each other. They gave us some situational questions, like "What would you do if you were stuck in the middle of Bangladesh with no money—how would you get out of the situation?" One of the things I do remember them asking is, "If only one of you could do the race, which one of you would do it?" I don't know where they were going with that—maybe to find out which one was going to be the leader of the two.

MR: After the interview, how did you feel you had done?

BS: I actually felt pretty confident. I think one of the things we realized—first of all being lawyers, second of all being young, athletic, good-looking guys—we knew if we were a bit cocky, that could help us out a little bit. In fact, I remember walking into the audition—it was in a hotel room, I had my briefcase—I walked in and said to one of the girls,

"Can you put this someplace for me?" I kind of came in with a smug personality right off the bat. Three girls interviewed us, and we had them laughing and smiling the whole time. I felt pretty confident afterwards.

A week or so later, they called us in to say that we'd made it into the final group of twenty-five teams, who were all flown into L.A. and put up in a hotel for around nine days. That's when you go through all the big tests. Psych tests, personality tests, IQ tests, and medical tests. I felt like I was taking the bar exam again. You're assigned times when you have to go down and eat, and you're just staring at all these people who might end up in your competition, and you can't talk to any of them. You're at their beck and call, waiting for them to say "Alright, come up to the presidential suite for a half hour, forty-five-minute interview, and then back down to your room." We just sat in our room waiting around, watching DVDs on the laptop. It was a pretty boring time.

Eventually you start your interviews with producers.

MR: Did you interview with Jerry Bruckheimer [one of the show's executive producers, and a famous film producer]?

BS: Jonathan Littman, his right-hand man, who is now an executive producer on the show, he was in all the interviews, as well as Bert van Munster, the co-creator and executive producer. . . . It was kind of intimidating. You walk in to these interviews and sometimes there's as many as ten people sitting there, waiting for you.

That went on for about a week, and at the end of the week they came to our room and said "OK, guys, we're taking you someplace." They wouldn't tell us where it was. They actually snuck us down in the service elevator, because the way this hotel was set up, if someone was down in the lobby, you could see who was going up and down in the elevators, so they didn't want anyone who wasn't going on this trip to see who was going. I think it was the final fourteen teams, and they put us in two separate vans, not allowed to talk—not even to each other—because people might be able to glean information off of you.

They drove us over to CBS; we met with Les Moonves [the head of CBS] and some of the other head honchos. I don't know if it's true or not, but supposedly out of those fourteen teams there were eleven they liked so much they couldn't pare it down to eight, and that's how they ended up doing eleven teams. I don't know if that's true—that could be an urban legend—but I know originally it was going to be eight teams and ended up being eleven.

MR: What was your strategy going into these big interviews?

BS: I think the biggest thing was just being ourselves. I knew we were a good team; I knew we were right for the show. Just being honest, and at the same time, try and understand what they want to hear. If you have to embellish a little bit, then embellish a little bit.

MR: Would you say you really tried to sell yourself?

BS: That's really what you're doing. You're selling yourself. When they asked, "Say you're in Italy, and you've got to quickly decide whether to take a train or a bus. What are you guys going to do?" Well, both Rob and I are type A personalities, we're both leaders, so we knew there were going to be times when we might butt heads, and we definitely played that up. We knew that was the kind of thing they were going to be looking for, but it's also the truth.

MR: How long after the finals did you find out you'd made the cut?

BS: Pretty soon. The last thing we did after that interview was come back and take final medical tests, and they gave us inoculations. We knew at that point we had well over a 50 percent shot at making the show. We knew we were pretty much on. They called and told us three days later.

MR: How do you feel having been on the show?

BS: The show itself was easily the most amazing experience of my life. It really was life-changing, and not necessarily in the way people think it would be. A lot of people would think the life-changing aspect was the fact that you were on national television and became famous for a while, that kind of thing. It really was more the experience of the race itself.

You end up becoming very close to people on your show. They're the only ones you can talk about it with. It was a very positive experience. I had traveled a bit before, but as far as traveling goes, it really gave me the travel bug. I've done a lot more traveling since coming back.

MR: How do you feel about how you were portrayed on the show?

BS: That was an interesting one. I think overall I was pleased with it, because we were a well-liked team—everyone was like, "Good guys do finish first." The thing that was a little bit strange to me was that, as I mentioned earlier, the things you get airtime for are being afraid, screwing up, and fighting. Well, Rob and I did none of the above, and because other teams did through the first half of the show, we didn't really get shown a whole lot.

We were portrayed as serious and a little bit quiet, and that's not how we are in real life. We just got edited that way, and me in particular. One of Rob's best friends from law school called me up and said, "I don't get it. In real life you're the one who does all the talking, and Rob's quiet. On the show, it's the opposite." That was a little frustrating, because you go on the Internet message boards and people say, "That guy Brennen never talked." But I guess it's much better than "Hey, that guy Brennen is an absolute asshole."

MR: Do you still watch the show?

BS: Absolutely. Complete fan of the show. If I had gotten turned on to it without having been on it, I think I'd still be a fan. I haven't missed one episode in six seasons. And I enjoy meeting people from the other seasons. There's so many people from all the reality shows, especially on CBS—we have nine seasons of *Survivor*, six seasons of *The Amazing Race*, five seasons of *Big Brother*. I've gone to *The Amazing Race* finale party for every season. It's kind of like a fraternity where each season we induct more people. I think that's why a lot of people on reality TV end up becoming friends: it's that shared experience.

Brennen is a lawyer living in Los Angeles, California.

THE APPRENTICE

The Apprentice **has had such a giant impact** on popular culture that I'm not even sure I'm allowed to say "You're Fired!" without getting sued. Every once in a while, a show comes along that hits home with the American people at exactly the right time and becomes an instant television phenomenon. First it was *Survivor*, then *American Idol*, and now *The Apprentice*.

From seasoned entrepreneurs to young go-getters with business savvy, every aspiring industrialist has dreamt of leaving a lasting impression on the world's most recognizable billionaire—or at least becoming his apprentice. Unfortunately, the more popular the show becomes, the harder it is to get cast. But I've put my nose to the grindstone to find out everything you need to know to maximize your chances of getting into that boardroom—thus getting you one step closer to hearing those magic words: "You're hired!"

STAT SHEET

PREMISE:
The best and brightest of the nation's business world battle it out for a chance to become iconic entrepreneur Donald Trump's apprentice—and the CEO of one of his companies.

HOST:
Donald Trump

NETWORK:
NBC

YEARS RUNNING:
Season 1 debuted in January of 2004.

CONTACT:
NBC—Web: *www.nbc.com*

PRODUCTION COMPANY:
Mark Burnett Productions

CREATOR:
Mark Burnett

EXECUTIVE PRODUCERS:
Mark Burnett, Donald Trump

CONTESTANT AGE RANGE:
21 and up

NUMBER OF APPLICANTS PER SEASON:
The show says over a million, but I'd put it closer to 100,000.

NUMBER OF CONTESTANTS CHOSEN:
Season 1 had sixteen contestants; Seasons Two and Three had eighteen contestants.

The Audition Process

The audition process for *The Apprentice* is a major undertaking for members of Mark Burnett's casting department, who travel all over the country interviewing tens of thousands of applicants and viewing tens of thousands of submitted videotapes. You'll have plenty of trouble standing out in the crowd among so many applicants, but failing to follow the correct auditioning procedures means you won't get seen at all. So before we put on our game faces, let's take a moment to learn the rules.

There are two ways onto *The Apprentice*: open calls and video applications.

Open Calls

Visit the NBC Web site (*www.nbc.com*) to find out if and when open calls have been scheduled for next season. Once you're at the call, the only thing you'll need is a completed application, which can be downloaded from the NBC Web site.

The application consists of basic questions about your career history and personal life. Some of its highlights include: "List your last three jobs and salary history" and "How would your co-workers describe you?" (I'd like to meet the person who answers that last question with "My coworkers think I'm lazy and stupid, and I believe each one of them is plotting my demise.") All applicants must be over 21 years of age and, while there's no specific age cutoff for applying, they've never cast anyone on the show in their 50s.

Even though there isn't much room for creativity on the application, do your best to stand out. Sticking to the obvious answers, like "My coworkers respect me as a leader and a friend," is something the casting directors see on thousands of applications. As is the case with all stages of *The Apprentice* casting process, do whatever it takes to stand out—in a good way. When the application asks for anecdotes from your life try to come up with something that they'll remember, something wild or funny. I'm not saying you should make these stories up, but using a bit of embellishment just to get your foot in the door never hurt anyone. At this stage in the audition process you just want to stand out and do what it takes (within reason) to get invited back for Round Two, where you'll be given an opportunity to really show them who you are.

The open call works much like your average job interview—that is, an average job interview in which plastic bracelets are handed out to thousands of people standing in massive lines outside of a convention center. Because of the show's popularity, the casting agents often don't have time to interview every person who shows up at an open call. Thus, the earlier you get in line, the better chance you have of getting seen. If the Web site tells you to start lining up at 8 A.M., start lining up at 6 A.M. You get only one shot at this, and there's no harm in sacrificing a little sleep for The Donald.

The casting agents spend the first two hours of each open call passing out wristbands, distributing short applications (for those who didn't bring their filled-out applications with them), and getting people into the proper order to begin interviews.

All interviews are conducted using the roundtable discussion method, in which ten potential cast members sit around a table and discuss questions posed to them by a member of the casting team. The questions usually relate to hot-button topics, for example, "Should prostitution be legalized?" or "Do you think lifelong monogamy is possible for most people?" Questions that get people arguing and speaking passionately are great ways for the casting people to quickly filter out the type A personalities from everyone else.

Video Application

Can't make it to an open call? No problem—just pull out your camcorder and get to work. Video applications must be *exactly* ten minutes long—no more and no less—and must be submitted on a VHS tape. Don't send in your mini-DV or Hi8 tapes: The casting team won't even watch them.

There isn't one right way to make a video application, but there are a lot of wrong ways. Don't play music in the background; don't backlight yourself so you appear on-screen in shadow; don't stand so far away from the camera that the casting agents can't see or hear you; and don't introduce the world to your pet— no one cares about Sparky. These seem like pretty obvious points, but you'd be surprised how many tapes get tossed after the first thirty seconds due to bad camera etiquette.

What you *should* do is take your viewers on a tour of your life. In the world of video applications, ten minutes is a lifetime—in fact, most reality shows allow video submissions of only three to five minutes. So if the casting team at *The Apprentice* wants to sit through ten minutes of pure *you*, those ten minutes had better be entertaining and chock-full of information. By the end of your tape, the casting agents should have a solid feel for your personality, a total understanding of your daily life—including, most important, your career—and some insight into your plans and aspirations for the future. Above all, your most important goal is to communicate why you believe you could be the next Apprentice: What skills do you have that separate you from everyone else? How would Donald Trump's organization benefit from having you as a part of its team?

Anyone with half a brain will try to hit these same points in his or her video application. This doesn't mean that you shouldn't hit these points—in fact, it's essential that you do. Rather, it means that you have to do it in a way that is completely memorable and entertaining. Imagine if you had to sit through thousands and thousands of hours of videotape. What would grab your attention? What would awaken you from your bleary-eyed stupor? Some people have gotten naked on their application tapes (not recommended), some have filmed their daily routines at work, some have reenacted scenes from past *Apprentice* episodes and shown how they could have done it better. There's no limit to what you can do on your videotape as long as it's creative and entertaining. It's your job to perk up that tired member of the casting department—to get him or her to watch your every move with bated breath. If you can do that, chances are good that you'll be called in for an interview.

Label both the front and spine of your VHS tape with your name, and with the number from the list below that corresponds to the city nearest you (or to which you'd prefer to travel if called for a Round Two interview).

MAIL THE ENTIRE PACKAGE, WITH YOUR SELF-DESIGNATED CITY NUMBER INCLUDED IN THE MAILING ADDRESS, TO:

★★★★★★★★★★★★★★★★★★★★★★

The Apprentice [City #]
914 Westwood Blvd #808
Los Angeles, CA 90024

★★★★★★★★★★★★★★★★★★★★★★

1. New York, NY
2. Los Angeles, CA
3. Chicago, IL
4. Tampa, FL
5. Washington, DC
6. Providence, RI
7. Atlanta, GA
8. Denver, CO
9. Seattle, WA
10. Phoenix, AZ
11. Raleigh-Durham, NC
12. Detroit, MI
13. Louisville, KY
14. San Jose, CA
15. Houston, TX
16. Kansas City, MO
17. Las Vegas, NV
18. Pittsburgh, PA
19. San Diego, CA
20. St. Louis, MO
21. Orlando, FL
22. Indianapolis, IN
23. Dallas, TX
24. Boise, ID
25. Albuquerque, NM
26. New Orleans, LA
27. Columbus, OH
28. Philadelphia, PA

In addition to your VHS tape and completed application, your application package must include proof of your eligibility to work in the U.S. (a photocopy of either a valid U.S. passport or a combination of a valid U.S. driver's license and a valid Social Security card).

Round Two and Beyond

The lucky little capitalists who make it to the next round (usually fewer than a thousand of the hundred thousand applicants who applied) will be asked to travel, at their own expense, to the cities they chose from the numbered list featured on the previous page. You'll also have to foot the bill for transportation and accommodations once you arrive in said city, so hopefully you didn't pick one too far away from where you live.

Before you arrive, you'll be sent a *gi-normous* application that requires information about nearly every imaginable facet of your life. Spend some extra time on the essay portions of this application. Provide specific examples from your life to illustrate how you've become the person you are today—the more memorable the stories you provide, the better. Your answers in this application will play a big part in your Round Two interview. Highlight your achievements in business, the obstacles you've had to overcome in life, and your ambitions for the future. A cast member in Season 3 told a story of how she spent a year of her life homeless yet was able to work her way out of it and become a successful entrepreneur. Stories like that really inspire a callback.

During Round Two, expect a thirty-minute, one-on-one taped interview with a casting associate or director. If you've put in the time with your application and come up with some great stories, this part should be a breeze, because they're going to ask you to recount some of those stories in a conversational manner. Since they're *your* stories, and no one in the world can tell them better than you, there should be nothing to worry about here. Just be natural and personable, and let the words flow as though you were Mark Twain himself.

Have you ever had a job interview in which you just *knew* that the interviewer was on your wavelength? In which the conversation flowed easily, and you could tell the interviewer was having a blast just talking to you? So much so that, when you left the office, you knew the job was in the bag, and you thought to yourself, "Man, if I can get this job, maybe I could get an even better job. Maybe I don't even want this job. I've totally underestimated my worth!" Yeah, that's kind of how you want this interview to go.

If you make it past this round, you'll be flown out to Hollywood for the finals, where the show's casting agents will turn you into a scientific research monkey and flog you with psychological evaluations, medical examinations, and background checks. You'll also be tossed to the lions in the form of countless interviews with casting directors, producers, and even the dreaded network executives (cue foreboding music).

If you can maintain your perma-smile (or evil scowl, depending on the role you're hoping to play on the show) and wow them with your countless business accolades and winning personality, you just may find yourself cast in the next season of *The Apprentice*.

Did You Know?

- Omarosa from Season 1 says the cartoon character to whom she most relates is Optimus Prime from *The Transformers*. Why, Omarosa? "Because he's the leader of the Transformers and works as a powerful force of goodness, courage, and wisdom in the battle against the evil Decepticons." Oh, I get it: You're crazy!

- The boardroom used by Mr. Trump to fire prospective Apprentices is not actually located at the top of Trump Tower. Rather, the boardroom set was built in the center of a large conference room in the building's lobby. All of the walls can be moved back and forth, and many of the wood panels are actually one-way mirrors, so the camera crew can get whatever shot or angle it needs. "Up to the suite, or down to the street?" More like, "Up to the suite, or... right out that door over there, down the hall, and make a left."

- Before appearing in (and winning) the first season of *The Apprentice*, Bill Rancic auditioned for *The Bachelor*.

WHAT THEY'RE LOOKING FOR

Let's cut right to the chase: *The Apprentice* is looking for young, smart, charismatic, up-and-coming entrepreneurs with the skills and leadership qualities necessary to run a major corporation. If you feel that you fit this bill to a T, your best bet is simply to be yourself, and make sure the casting team knows how badly you want to be a part of its show. This is what we call "being real."

On the other hand, the producers also want people who embody certain roles. They want the small-town guy with a high school education; the cold-hearted businesswoman from Washington, D.C.; the crazy, willing-to-do-anything businessman; and the young, handsome entrepreneur. When they meet with you, the producers are hoping to cast you in a highly specific role on their show. Your job is to paint for them a picture of who this character will be, and what part he or she will play—and, once you've painted that picture, to *stick to it*.

I can't stress this enough: The casting agents *hate* wishy-washy people. They want you to believe in yourself and be willing to fight (though not literally) for your beliefs against any who might challenge you. And, although most people are pretty multifaceted, they're not so interested in that. Rather, they want you to show your strongest side, your most entertaining side, and then display that side consistently for the entire time you're on camera.

It's a balancing act that few can juggle, but knowing what they're looking for will give you an edge that most others are lacking.

Be honest. Be real. Be bigger than life. Be consistent.

Once your tape is chosen, make this your mantra through the next few phases of the audition. Next thing you know, you could be unpacking your bags in Trump Plaza.

Interview
Stacy Rotner, *The Apprentice 2*

MR: How did you find out about the *Apprentice* casting call?

SR: I saw the advertisement on TV. I had really enjoyed the first season, so I went online and got all the information. I knew they required a video submission, but I didn't have time for that, so I ended up going to the open casting call in New York.

MR: What was the casting call like?

SR: Well, I stood outside in the snow for four hours. (Laughs.) It was intense. Ultimately, they were looking for someone who stood out as a personality. You can't be middle-of-the-road; you have to take a position and you have to be memorable.

MR: What do you think you did at the audition that helped you get cast on the show?

SR: Being extremely opinionated and outspoken was crucial. You also have to wear something that's memorable. I think the whole key to auditioning is to try and be memorable, and to stand out, and also to be yourself—because ultimately that's who you're going to have to be on the show.

MR: How do you feel about how you were portrayed on the show?

SR: I think that they took pieces of me and made them extreme. Obviously there was a lot of editing that took place. They can't show all of everyone, so they have to show snippets. Unfortunately, they're most likely going to end up showing a lot more negative than positive. Look, I'm a lawyer, so the fact that they characterized me as argumentative and opinionated and inquisitive wasn't the worst thing. It didn't hurt my career.

MR: When you first went in to audition, how did you pitch yourself?

SR: Well, at the open call we all sat on a panel.

MR: Would you say you were the most outspoken person on your panel?

SR: Definitely. At one point, someone chimed in while I was talking, and I shot him a look and said "Don't interrupt me. Let me finish what I'm saying." I think it's saying things like that that ultimately translate into you standing out as an individual.

I was myself to an extreme. The way to pitch yourself is not to list the traits that characterize you—it's more about telling stories that depict the person that you are. Instead of saying "I'm really outgoing and opinionated," give examples of how you're outgoing and opinionated in your life. That shines through much more than just describing yourself.

I gave examples of myself in law school and in my social life—examples of how I'm a leader, how my character traits relate to me.

MR: How long was the whole audition process?

SR: A little over a month. I had to take off two months from work, but I was really excited to be on the show. It was a great experience. It was a unique, once-in-a-lifetime experience. I didn't do it to be famous. I did it for the game and for the experience and to see if it would open interesting doors and opportunities, and it has. To that end, I'm really pleased that I did it.

MR: What advice would you give someone who wanted to get on *The Apprentice*?

SR: Stand out, be memorable, take a position, and know who you are and why you're going in there. Otherwise you just blend. For *The Apprentice*, they're looking for someone who's intelligent, with some business acumen—with skills that translate well in the work world.

When you're vying for a position to work for someone, whether it's Donald Trump or Martha Stewart, you need to be able to speak to what appeals to them. As a lawyer, I think that building a case as to why you would be a good employee is really what you need to be heading for. Treat the whole process like a job interview.

Stacy currently works at a large law firm in New York City. She makes regular public-speaking, radio, and television appearances and also provides legal commentary. For more on Stacy, visit www.stacyrotner.com.

BIG BROTHER

Standing out from the crowd: A man dressed as a Roman gladiator at a March 2004 *Big Brother* open call audition in Birmingham, England (Photo by Dee Custance)

STAT SHEET

PREMISE:
One house. A group of strangers. One hundred days. Dozens of cameras. Hundreds of microphones. Every moment captured on video. No contact with the outside world. No luxuries. Who will outlast the others to win $500,000? You will decide.

HOST:
Julie Chen

NETWORK:
CBS

YEARS RUNNING:
Season 1 premiered in the U.S. in 2000. The final episode of Season 5 aired in September of 2004.

CONTACT:
CBS—Web: *www.cbs.com*

PRODUCTION COMPANY:
CBS

CREATOR:
John De Mol

EXECUTIVE PRODUCERS:
Don Wollman, Allison Grodner, Arnold Shapiro, Paul Romer, Douglas Ross, Greg Stewart, J. Rupert Thompson

CONTESTANT AGE RANGE:
21 and up

NUMBER OF APPLICANTS PER SEASON:
20,000

NUMBER OF CONTESTANTS CHOSEN:
The producers change it up from season to season, but somewhere between ten and fourteen is a safe bet.

What is there to say about *Big Brother*? It was there when the reality TV phenomenon began, and it's still there today. In the beginning it seemed so simple: Stick a bunch of people in a house, film their every move, and wait as one by one they begin to crack. The whacko who can stand the cameras and the cabin fever the longest wins half a million bucks.

The first few seasons were exciting, innovative, and even—dare I say?—naughty. I miss the days of knife-wielding white rappers, pixilated body parts, and twenty-four-hour uncensored Internet voyeurism where you never knew what was going to happen next. The past few seasons have felt more like a congressional hearing interspersed with wacky games and arbitrary contests. Well, consider this a call to arms, my reality TV–loving brethren! Read this chapter, follow its instructions, get cast on *Big Brother*, and save this show! Get naked, get crazy, get arrested-just do something to spice up this show and return it to its glorious roots. Hallelujah!

The Audition Process

CBS has its own casting style—a style it originated with *Survivor*, passed on to *Big Brother*, and continues to use today with *The Amazing Race*. It's a fast, no-frills audition process that attracts the widest possible group of auditioners without forcing the network to spend too much time on any one applicant.

During a CBS audition, you get two minutes to strut your stuff—and that's all anyone will see of you unless and until you're picked for the semifinals. The CBS two-minute formula means that the casting people know what they want, and if you can't deliver it spot-on within two minutes, you're out of luck. That's the bad news. But there's also good news: The fact that CBS always uses the same formula also means that you know what they want, which puts you one step ahead of the game! Check the technique.

Before you do anything else, find out if the show is casting. You can check *CBS.com* for up-to-date information—if it's casting, the network will advertise this fact prominently on its Web page. Click on the *Big Brother* icon and download an application and instructions on where to send a tape or attend an open casting call.

In addition, stay tuned to CBS during prime time (no, I don't work for CBS). If there's a casting call being held in your area, your local CBS network affiliate will usually run a "crawl"—a small line of information that scrolls across the bottom of the TV screen—letting you know where and when to find an audition.

Video Application

Pull out your video camera, sit your butt down on your couch, start your stopwatch, and give CBS your best possible two minutes. The main topic of your self-interview should be "Why I think I should be a house guest on the next *Big Brother*." But somehow, in the process of answering that question, you also have to provide a clear and concise idea of who you are and what role you're going to play in the house. Here's a quote straight from the horse's patoot (i.e., from one of *Big Brother*'s casting directors):

> The best tapes are the ones with people just sitting on their couches showing us their personalities. We want to see how much fun they can have—we want to see what they're like, what they do, where they're from. We want those two minutes to be chock-full of information about

themselves, who they are, and why they would make a great competitor—because that's what *Big Brother* is all about: strategy and competition. Also, we love hearing some criticism, too: what they thought of past *Big Brother* players, what they did wrong, and then what they think they could have done better.

Which leads me to an important point: Know the show. Be an expert. Know all the characters' names, know the past dramas. Refer to them in your tape. In terms of strategy, the producers want you to bring something *new* to the show—something they've never seen before. Make sure you have a game plan going in, and make sure you communicate that game plan in your tape.

Another tip the casting director gave me is that the casting team really isn't looking for people who just want to be on TV or get famous. That's a *big* turnoff for casting directors. Don't say that you were born to be a star, and that you hope *Big Brother* will catapult you into the acting career for which you've always been destined. You can think that in your head if you like, but keep it to yourself on your two-minute tape.

One last tip: If you can think of something that separates you from the pack—some special talent, skill, or passion you have—let them see it. Spend the first minute or minute and a half of your video application sitting on your couch talking about yourself. Then, if you're a pro skater, show them a few tricks. If you're a rapper (see the interview with Mike Boogie on page 125), write them a little rap. If you're a wild and crazy person, do something wild and crazy! It never hurts to "wow" them in the end—just don't spend the whole time being crazy. Make sure they see your "real" side first.

Next, download the long application from *www.cbs.com*. As always, don't provide any one-word answers to the questions on the application—the longer, the better. Each answer should be a short essay. Don't ramble on for the sake of filling up space, but make sure you cram in every bit of information about yourself that you possibly can so the casting team can get a clear idea of who you are. The application should take you about an hour to complete.

Then find a point-and-shoot camera and take two good photos of yourself to include with your application: a full-body shot and a head-and-shoulders shot. You'll also need a photocopy of some form of real identification: either a driver's license or a passport.

Open Casting Calls

A quick tip before you show up at the open call: The casting people will need two pictures of you to attach to your application. You can either take them yourself—with good lighting, a nice camera, and while making a nice face—and bring them with you to the open call, or you can let some intern with a Polaroid—someone who's taken four thousand other photos that day—take the *only* photo of you the CBS executives may ever see. You've seen the photo on your driver's license, right? Bottom line: Bring your own pictures.

ATTACH THE PHOTOCOPY AND PHOTOS TO YOUR APPLICATION AND MAIL EVERYTHING TO:

★★★★★★★★★★★★★★★★★★★★★★★★

Big Brother [Region #]
P.O. Box 520
11271 Ventura Blvd
Studio City, CA 91604

★★★★★★★★★★★★★★★★★★★★★★★★

Your region number corresponds to the city listed below that is closest to your home:

01. *New York, NY*	07. *Chicago, IL*
02. *Pittsburgh, PA*	08. *Memphis, TN*
03. *Boston, MA*	09. *Minneapolis, MN*
04. *Atlanta, GA*	
05. *Los Angeles, CA*	10. *Dallas, TX*
	11. *Miami, FL*
06. *Denver, CO*	12. *Seattle, WA*

Along the same lines, the application you'll fill out at the open call is the same application you can download from the CBS Web site. So save yourself an hour: Fill it out before you come and bring it with you.

Most *Big Brother* casting calls take place at local CBS affiliate stations (the same places that local CBS newscasts are filmed). Occasionally, however, casting calls are held in local hotel banquet halls. Once again, check the CBS Web site for up-to-the-minute information.

As far as I know (and I know pretty far in the world of reality-TV casting), CBS is the only network that conducts one-on-one interviews at open casting calls—unlike the roundtable style used by Bunim/Murray and most other reality shows. The casting director described the interview process to me as "the same thing as your two-minute video, but done live right in front of us." Since the casting agents will also be filming you while they talk to you, the open casting call is basically just for people who don't have access to video cameras, or for people who love standing in lines (you know who you are).

In your interview, the casting agents will prompt you with the same two questions you'd be expected to answer in a videotaped application: "Why do you want to be on *Big Brother*?" and "What would be your strategy in the house?" Just like in the video application, you're gonna want to squeeze in as much personal information about yourself as possible, while at the same time answering those questions. At the two-minute mark, the interviewers will thank you for your time and send you on your way, keeping your two photos and application for further review. And that's it.

Round Two and Beyond

Big Brother casts in twelve regions throughout the country. The cities in those regions vary from season to season, but you can bet that Los Angeles, New York City, and Las Vegas will always be well-mined. Once the casting team has compiled everyone's videotapes, applications, and photos (both sent-in and taken from open calls), they'll whittle down the thousands and thousands of applicants to a group of fifty from each region, for a grand total of six hundred people. And how do they go all the way from tens of thousands to six hundred? Magic. Dark magic. Either that or they just work really hard—I'm not sure.

The fifty applicants selected from each region are then invited to thirty-minute one-on-one interviews at their local CBS affiliates. The thirty-minute interview is an in-depth version of the two-minute interview. Expect to talk about nearly every facet of your life, while providing your interviewer with even more reasons why you'd make an exemplary *Big Brother* contestant. And whatever you do, don't clam up. The casting directors tell me that tons of people—all of whom showed so much potential in their two-minute videos—clam up during these interviews, giving only one- or two-word answers. That type of interview usually doesn't last longer than five minutes. There are no second chances, so be your biggest and most personable self.

After the local interviews, the final six hundred applicants are pared down to a lucky group of fifty potential contestants, all of whom are flown out to Los Angeles and put up in a hotel for up to ten days (depending on how far each person advances in the process). At this point, the casting directors will inform you that "the game has already begun"—meaning you aren't allowed to tell *anyone* why you're going to Los Angeles for ten days. If you *need* to tell someone—like your spouse or parents or boss—CBS will demand that your confidants sign a confidentiality agreement. If they were to breach this agreement, they could be sued for up to $5 million. I'm not kidding. This is serious business.

Once in L.A, you'll undergo extensive psychological and medical testing and conduct dozens of interviews with casting directors, producers, and sometimes network executives. During this process, you will not be allowed to talk to, consort with, or make eye contact with any other potential cast members—the producers don't want anyone forging early alliances! As one casting director put it, "If they're getting into an elevator and see someone who they think might be a *Big Brother* finalist, they are to let it go and wait for the next one. It is strict."

Here's another interesting fact to keep in mind if you make it to the final group of fifty: Each finalist has a "handler" who acts as his or her escort for the final stages of the casting process. Your handler will be the *only* person, aside from the casting directors and network execs, with whom you will be allowed to have contact. You'll do *everything* with this person: eat all your meals, go to the gym—basically everything other than sit in your room and wait. Most likely, you will become friends with this person . . . but watch your back!

Your handler isn't just some intern assigned to babysit you—far from it. In fact, time spent with your handler is considered one of the most important phases of the casting process. Surprise, surprise: Your handler is a casting agent! He or she will report your every move and word back to the casting directors. If you pass another finalist in the hall and say "She's got fake boobs . . . I just know it," your handler will report back to the casting directors that you're "catty" and "competitive," which will cause the casting directors to smile mischievously, rub their hands together, and whisper "Excellent" to themselves in ominous tones. OK, maybe that's not their exact response, but you get the picture. They're keeping tabs on you, so watch what you say! Make sure you stay in character!

After that, it's all in the hands of the network executives! Good luck!

Did You Know?

The voice of *Big Brother*, Julie Chen, recently became the wife of *Big Brother* when she married the head of CBS: Les Moonves. Looks like the show might stick around a few more years.

WHAT THEY'RE LOOKING FOR

The casting directors told me that a great *Big Brother* contestant is someone with "attitude, competitiveness, aggressiveness. They have nothing but each other in the house, so if you get a bunch of boring people in there, it will be a dreadfully boring show. You want people who will stir the pot—who won't be afraid to stand up for themselves, to compete, to be hard-core competitors."

At the same time—and these are all my own deductions—there seems to be a very direct formula used on *Big Brother* (and on many reality shows, though *Big Brother* provides the most consistent examples). The show always seems to feature certain specific types of "characters": a New York/East Coast character; a strong, black character; a strong, gay character; hot leading male and hot leading female characters; and an old curmudgeonly character, to name a few. Then there are always a few "X-factor" characters thrown into the mix—people who break the mold and add something new and fresh to the show each season.

The lesson to be learned from this? If you don't fit any of these "character" types, you need to figure out who *your* character will be, and what you'll bring to the show in terms of personality and strategy. And then you need to stick to that character type 24/7. (See my interview with *Big Brother* 2's Mike "Boogie" Malin, below, for more information on character development.)

While most reality shows look only for type A personalities, *Big Brother* is willing to branch out a bit and cast what one casting director referred to as a "strong, silent type." There are people who aren't typical type A personalities, but who are nonetheless competitive, though in a quieter way. Jason and Lisa, who went on to win *Big Brother 3*, are good examples. They had what the casting directors refer to as "quiet strength."

In the end, the casting directors told me, "we want people who really want to compete and play the game. *Big Brother* is all about the game."

Interview
Mike Malin (aka "Mike Boogie"), *Big Brother 2*

MR: What made you want to audition for *Big Brother*?

MM: My inspiration for being on a reality TV show was watching the cast of *Survivor 1*, and seeing these people who were in fashion school, and selling insurance in Ohio, and now they're on the red carpet, doing guest spots on sitcoms, and doing commercials. I thought, "I'm an actor, casting directors already know who I am, I have a great agent. What could I do with that exposure?"

At that time [2001], there was no other game in town. There was no *For Love or Money*, there was no *Average Joe*. It was *Survivor* and *Big Brother*. They were casting *Survivor 3* and *Big Brother 2* simultaneously. I basically thought to myself, "OK, I'm gonna make a tape. But what's my angle? There's gonna be a million people in their late twenties, early thirties. Everyone's going to be outgoing with a big personality. What are my 'hooks'?"

The first thing I thought of was my occupation. There are very few young people that own a bar. There are very few people who understand how the process [of network television] works. I decided to basically craft a character, as an actor.

I created this character, "Mike Boogie," which is what my friends called me—the whole rapping, sports-jersey-with-the-visor-on [guy]. I knew that would separate me—not only from the pretty boys, but from the other guys that were supposedly the frat guys, party guys, whatever that role is: the troublemakers.

Photo courtesy of Mike Malin

So my basic angle with the tape was to do a dance. I remember it was to Janet Jackson's "All for You" single, and I did a whole dancing montage. I had my video editor friend cut it up like a real demo reel, because everyone else would send in grainy home videos and I knew it would catch their eye if I did something with music and good cinematography.

At the end of the montage, I did a rap about why *Big Brother 1* sucked, why it didn't work. I rapped about really insider things: target demographics, things that I knew nobody in the country would know about. I said to myself, "They don't want the inaudible 'wigger,'" if you will. So I hit them with, "I own this bar, I'm an articulate graduate of an East Coast private college," just to show them my different shades. Basically, when you go in as an actor, when you audition, they don't want one note, so that's what I didn't give them.

MR: And how did you hear about the opportunity to send in a tape? How did you know they were casting?

MM: The casting directors came into my bar and they said "You should send in a tape because you've got a colorful personality."

MR: So when you sent your tape in, did it go in with the general population's tapes, or did you have a special hookup because the casting people had come into your bar?

MM: I told them the day I was making it and when I was sending it in, and they said they'd look for it, but I thought they were just kissing ass to get a free martini at the time. I think it went in with everyone else's tape.

I knew there was no way, from a casting perspective, I could compete with the good-looking guys. I knew I wasn't the frat guy, I knew I wasn't the gay guy, I wasn't the hick. My thing was the "big-city party guy who gets it." Maybe not the best-looking, but not the worst-looking. He's the fun guy you want to go out and party with.

I knew they wanted character development, especially with *Big Brother*, where there's no picturesque scenery, there's no crazy contests, it's all about the people. But you can't watch a fun guy the whole time—you can't watch a guy having a great time all the time, because nobody's lives are like that all the time.

In my real life, I had never met my father. I knew it would come up [in the interview], and I think I answered one of the questions on the questionnaire in a way that would solicit their asking about it. I just started crying in the interview when they brought it up. I wanted them to think, "Jesus, we put this party boy in the house and in week two we actually get him to break down crying. What a diverse character that is!"

About a month later, I got a call that I was to check into the Sheraton Universal for eight days of interviews. I had made it to the final fifty.

At the hotel, they put you in this room. You have escorts at all times. You're not allowed to talk to any other potential contestants, but you see them with guys with walkie-talkies, so you know who the other people are. So for those eight days, you're sizing people up.

MR: And you're completely sequestered because they don't want you forming alliances with other people, right?

MM: Right. But I had already formed in my head the people that I could tell were probably gonna get picked. You'd see them by the pool: the country hottie, the old curmudgeon guy.

During the final fifty, I could see the numbers were dwindling come day six, day seven. So I wrote another rap, tailor-made for the producers. On the eighth day, they put nine guys in one van and nine girls in another van and we weren't allowed to talk to each other, and I knew where we were going. We were going to see Les Moonves [the head of CBS]. I just knew it.

I had a sense that this was it, this was my big moment, and it was such a range of emotions because I wasn't even that excited about being on *Big Brother*—I was excited about what *Big Brother* was gonna do for me. And so I wrote a rap tailor-made for Les Moonves and this final audition.

I went in, and all the executives were there. Les sat in the middle like it was his, like, royal court, and he asked me, "Can you rap a little?" So I did this whole rap that was like, "I am right here with you, and I know what this show means to your summer network schedule, and I will be your guy. I'm gonna be your point guard in the house, I'm gonna help you create story lines, and I'm gonna stir it up when it needs to be stirred up. You want me in this house."

Also, I had played up the sex angle, like I was gonna [sleep with] every girl in the house. I'm not even that much of a ladies' man, but I knew that was part of what they wanted to see. So [one of the network executives] asked, "What makes you think you're gonna sleep with a girl in the house this summer?" And I was like, "All due respect, but I own the hottest bar in L.A. I sometimes sleep with two girls a night. I'm not that worried about it."

My point being, if you apply on a reality TV show, you better have every angle covered. You can never hesitate on an answer—you have to act like you're marching to your own drummer. In the back of my mind, I'm going, "I'm in front of these people who can snap their fingers and put me in front of 15 million people, and I need to answer every question right on point."

About two weeks later, they called me and said "We want to film a thing at your bar in case you get picked." I knew the cast was already picked at that point—they weren't going to just send a crew [for no reason].

They showed up at my bar that night, and they filmed it like it wasn't really happening, and then all of a sudden they gave me the key to the house and I had to drive home, pack my suitcase, which was already packed, and check back into the Sheraton Universal—except this time without a computer, without a TV. It was real lockdown, because they were gonna start running the promos and we were gonna go into the house in five days. So we had to spend five days in that hotel—couldn't even see any of the other contestants, weren't allowed to do anything. And then they just dropped us in the house and we did the show.

MR: You said you were kind of playing a character when you auditioned. You said you knew what they wanted to see. Describe your character for me.

MM: I remember a few times they referred to me as "the rapping Beverly Hills bar owner." It's the party guy, the fun guy, the guy who gets the party started. I mean, who doesn't want to own a bar at thirty years old? I was the guy that first night who got everyone to drink beers and get in the hot tub and lick whipped cream off each other. I went through that whole [audition] process with a very strict agenda—with a lot of knowledge about how things work. And, you know, it all went according to plan.

I remember meeting Will Kirby the first night [in the *Big Brother* house], who ended up winning, and I was like, "Oh my god, there's someone here who gets it as much as I do." So we got together and I said "Look, you get with that girl Shannon. You're gonna be the reality prom king and queen of the summer. I'm gonna get with the other one. We'll have this, like, double-date romance throughout the summer." Which is very passé now, but four years ago there was no *Bachelor*, *Average Joe*, *For Love or Money*—the whole romance thing, you had never seen that on reality TV at that point.

I remember coaxing people. I was trying to get some drinking game going, and people were like, "No, we're just gonna play cards." And I was like, "Really? Nicole, you told me you wanted your own cooking show. Well, you're not gonna get it playing cards. We gotta get naked, we gotta fight. That's what we gotta do if you guys want these things afterwards."

I remember in *Entertainment Weekly* they wrote how Will and I were "hyper-aware of our TV personas," and we were.

MR: Looking back on the experience—the casting and the actual show—how do you feel about it?

MM: The casting experience could not have gone better. It was perfect. I've probably never set out to do anything in my life that worked so according to plan with not a bump in the road.

The actual experience of being there was absolutely miserable. I've never felt so stressed and fragile, with my mind kind of freaked out and bored and all these things that I don't want to encompass in my everyday life.

MR: What advice would you give someone who wanted to be on not just *Big Brother*, but any reality TV show?

MM: Do it for the right reasons. Do it for the actual experience. If you don't think you want to sit in a backyard for a month, don't apply to *Big Brother*. If you don't think you can eat sand or ants and be away from your husband, don't apply for *Survivor*. Go do something you want to do. If you want to be the next model, go be on *America's Next Top Model*. If you want to test yourself and starve yourself and have this physical challenge, apply to *Survivor*.

But blowing up after a reality show is over. I don't care who you are—if you think you're gonna go on *The Real World* or *Road Rules* and blow up, you're not. You're gonna go do two college appearances for a grand each, and then you're gonna work at the Saddle Ranch for eight bucks an hour. It's reality.

My thing is, do it for the right reasons, but be cautious. Because getting that little moment can be very intoxicating, and when it's gone it can be the worst hangover of your life.

The aftereffect initially was such an extreme letdown for me. I knew it wasn't going to be *Survivor*—with my knowledge of the industry, I understood the differences between sweeps programs and July alternative programming. I didn't walk out of the house and expect to host *Saturday Night Live*. But I certainly expected to have more opportunities than were there. I have to say though, three years later, I pat myself on the back because I was able to overcome that disappointment and do a lot. You know that axiom of fifteen minutes of fame? Well, there is no one that stretched it further than me.

Mike Malin is currently continuing his career as a successful restaurant entrepreneur in Los Angeles. He owns some of the most popular, celebrity-filled restaurants in town, including Dolce, The Geisha House, and The Lodge in Hollywood, CA.

THE BIGGEST LOSER

STAT SHEET

PREMISE:
Twelve overweight contestants battle it out to see who can lose the most weight, win the cash prize, and be crowned The Biggest Loser.

HOST:
Caroline Rhea

NETWORK:
NBC

YEARS RUNNING:
Season 1 first aired in October of 2004.

CONTACT:
Web: *www.nbc.com/The_Biggest_Loser/*

PRODUCTION COMPANY:
3Ball Productions

EXECUTIVE PRODUCERS:
J. D. Roth, Todd A. Nelson, Ben Silverman, David Broome, John Foy

CONTESTANT AGE RANGE:
21 and up

NUMBER OF APPLICANTS PER SEASON:
20,000

NUMBER OF CONTESTANTS CHOSEN:
Twelve per season

Let the reality-TV weight loss phenomenon begin! Thanks to the popularity of the first season of *The Biggest Loser*, we all have the pleasure of staring at fat people on our TVs every night. I'm just kidding. But in all seriousness, *The Biggest Loser* was the total sleeper hit of fall 2004—an interesting, emotional series that came out of left field and surprised everyone, and will likely have strong legs for several years to come.

Not many shows can, in the course of a mere thirteen episodes, go from being called one of the most tasteless reality shows ever to being praised as one of the most positive shows on TV. I would have figured that watching people lose weight would be about as interesting as watching paint dry, but somehow *The Biggest Loser* is able to pull you in and get you involved emotionally with each cast member's weight loss struggle. Which gets many of you horizontally-challenged folks out there thinking: "Could I be the Biggest Loser?"

The Audition Process

You've seen the show, you've got a few pounds to lose, and you feel that the best way to lose that weight is in front of a few million people? Well, I've got all the info you need--so go grab a sandwich, run (or shuffle) back, and let's get started. Tally ho!

There are two ways to land a spot on *The Biggest Loser*: through open calls and video applications.

Open Calls

The Biggest Loser uses the roundtable auditioning method in its open casting calls, wherein four or five people sit at a table and field questions from a casting director. Each applicant then has the opportunity to answer the questions, or argue with someone else about his or her answers. The Golden Rule of roundtable auditions is this: The squeaky wheel gets oiled. Meaning, do whatever it takes to get the casting directors' attention, and hold onto that attention for dear life.

The people I talked to who auditioned for *The Biggest Loser* at an open casting call said that most of the questions asked by the casting directors focused on how committed they were to losing weight. Lizzeth, who was cast on Season 1 of *The Biggest Loser*, responded to this question at her open casting call by saying "I want my butt kicked. If I don't make it on the show, I'm going to join the military just for the boot camp so I can get my butt kicked. I'm looking for someone to beat the crap out of me. I want to puke. I want my body to shake because of how hard I'm working out. I'm looking to go balls-out."

Although Lizzeth admitted she wasn't the most outspoken person at her roundtable, she was—obviously—the most graphic in her descriptions of how badly she wanted to lose weight. The reason she was selected over the other people at her table—even those who spoke more than she did—was that her answers were more memorable. The lesson here is that, although the squeaky wheel always gets oiled, the Golden Rule doesn't necessarily require you to be the loudest or most talkative person at your audition table. Rather, leaving a lasting impression on the casting director is the most important requirement for making it to Round Two.

Video Application

If you can't make it down to an open call, your best bet is to create your own videotaped application. Tapes should be between five and ten minutes in length, and in VHS format.

There are many theories as to what makes a great video application. But no matter what show you're applying for, the same core principles apply: be yourself, let your personality shine through, and tug on the heartstrings whenever possible. In addition, you'll want to address a few specific topics in your video application for *The Biggest Loser*

★ Talk about your lifelong struggle with weight loss. At what age did you become overweight? How did it affect your life while growing up? How have you struggled with dieting and exercise?

★ Explain how losing weight would change your life. What is your motivation for wanting to lose weight? What doors would open in your life if you were thinner?

★ If you were cast on the show, how would you go about becoming The Biggest Loser? How driven are you to lose the most weight?

The reason *The Biggest Loser* is regarded as one of the most positive reality shows on TV is that each cast member's weight loss journey is both emotional and inspiring. If you want to be cast on *The Biggest Loser*, you've got to figure out the key factor that motivates you to lose weight—and how that's going to translate into an inspiring story on-screen. Whether you're motivated by a desire to gain the self-confidence you've always lacked, or to stick around long enough to watch your kids grow up, you've got to give the casting department a story it can grab onto and run with.

While not every person cast on *The Biggest Loser* has a sob story motivating his or her weight loss, the majority of cast members are selected because they *needed* to lose weight more than any of the other contestants who auditioned. Unless you take the Aaron Semel route (see my interview with Aaron at the end of this chapter) and establish yourself as the guy (or gal) whose role on the show is to lighten things up so they don't get too depressing, you're going to have to show the casting department that you deserve to be on the show more than all of the other overweight people in this country.

Round Two and Beyond

If the casting department likes your application, two things will begin to happen: Casting directors will begin to pitch your story to the show's producers, and they'll start calling you for more information. You'll be sent a long application, which asks about a zillion questions regarding every facet of your life—from your medical records to your romantic history. You'll also be asked to do a handful of phone interviews with the casting associates so they can get to know you better and ask any unanswered questions they have about you. If you don't live in the Los Angeles area, you may also be asked to film yourself during these phone interviews and send the tapes to the casting department. This process lasts anywhere from a few weeks to a few months.

ONCE YOU'VE COMPLETED YOUR TAPE, DOWNLOAD AND COMPLETE THE SHORT APPLICATION (AVAILABLE AT WWW.NBC.COM/THE_BIGGEST_LOSER/) AND MAIL THE WHOLE PACKAGE TO:

★★★★★★★★★★★★★★★★★★★★★★

3Ball Productions
Attn: *Biggest Loser* Casting
1600 Rosecrans Avenue
Building 7, 2nd Floor
Manhattan Beach, CA 90266

★★★★★★★★★★★★★★★★★★★★★★

If you make it to the final stage of the casting process, which lasts about a week, you'll be flown out to Los Angeles and put up in a hotel. During this time you'll undergo medical and psychological testing, as well as an extensive background check. All finalists are sequestered in their hotel rooms until called for interviews and are blindfolded (!) while being driven to and from the studio to meet with producers and network executives—all to keep any potential castmates from sizing up (no pun intended) the competition or forming early alliances.

After the finals, you'll find out within a few days whether you've been selected to appear on the show.

Did You Know?

The first season's cast of *The Biggest Loser* was faced with a termite infestation in the house that was never shown on camera. Apparently it was such a big deal that a few members of the cast had to sleep on couches for three or four days while they waited for exterminators to take care of the infestation. At least something in the house was eating as much as it wanted.

WHAT THEY'RE LOOKING FOR

Aaron Semel, a cast member from Season 1 of *The Biggest Loser*, told me a story that I think speaks volumes about what the show is looking for in its future contestants.

The week of the live taping of the Season 1 finale, the entire cast met up in Los Angeles for an untaped get-together at a local restaurant. This was the first time the whole cast had ever hung out together outside of the show—and, for most of them, the first time they had had a chance to interact with each other without any cameras around. When I asked Aaron to describe the dinner for me, he summed it up in one word: "loud." He explained:

Each one of these people is probably considered "the loud one" in their group of friends. They're probably all the life of the party wherever they go. Now imagine getting all of those types of people together in one place and time for dinner. It was very loud. I found it hard to get a word in edgewise, and I consider myself a loud person.

The moral of the story is this: *The Biggest Loser* wants people who are *big*. . . in *every* sense of the word. They want charismatic, outgoing, and candid individuals who aren't afraid to speak their minds, and who wear their hearts on their sleeves.

As for the show's physical requirements, obviously you have to be overweight to be cast, but you don't have to be obese. Whether you weigh 400 pounds or 250 pounds, if you have a memorable personality and a strong conviction to lose weight, you'll be in a good position to do well in the casting process.

Interview
Aaron Semel, *The Biggest Loser 1*

MR: How did you find out they were casting for *The Biggest Loser*?

AS: I was looking for a job on craigslist [a popular Web site] every day, and there was a posting that said "Do you want to lose forty to sixty pounds on a major network reality show?" I was like, "I can do that!" I was about 240 pounds then, so I thought "If I lose forty pounds, I would only weigh 200 pounds. That would be great. I can totally do that."

I sent them an E-mail that described my whole life story in three paragraphs. I talked about how I was a skinny kid who got fat, then I lost the weight after college because I ran triathlons, but now I'm getting fat again. I was really trying to hone in on their emotional side by making it seem like it was my life quest to be skinny.

They called me a week later and asked me a bunch of questions on the phone for half an hour, and then asked me to come in for an interview. When I went in for the interview, I saw this hot chick talking on her cell phone in the NBC parking lot. I walked by and said "hello," kind of flirting with her. I get upstairs and it turns out I just flirted with Alison Kass, the casting coordinator for *The Biggest Loser*.

I was wearing a suit to the interview because auditioning for *The Biggest Loser* was just one of the job interviews I had that day. It's funny to call it a "job interview," since it's a reality-TV casting call, but that's how I was treating it.

Alison Kass comes up to me in the lobby upstairs, and I totally felt like she was flirting with me. So I flirted back, and then they called me into my interview, where I was disappointed to find there was another casting person doing the interview.

The questions all seemed to be about finding an emotional tie to being fat. Questions like, "What was it like being fat in high school?" "Are any relationships in your life affected by your weight?" Stuff like that. They were also trying to get information on why I was fat. They asked me what my favorite foods were, and what my biggest temptations were. That was it.

After that they sent me home and asked me to make a ten-minute video. They told me to have a friend follow me around with a video camera and show them my life. I had just seen a video a friend of mine had done to audition for *The Apprentice*, and I thought it was perfect, so I basically copied it.

I wrote a seven-page script with an intro, a middle, and an end. I spent about three days making the video. Basically the video begins with me on my rooftop, in a suit, looking over downtown L.A. I tried to make it funny. I started with "I'm Aaron Semel, I live in Los Angeles, I'm originally from Chicago, and I'm fat." And then I cut to a shot of me dancing in a Speedo bikini and my body covered in tribal paint. So I'm cutting back and forth between me on the roof in a suit explaining why I'm fat to me dancing half-naked in a Speedo to techno music.

From there I went on to "A Day in the Life of Me." I showed my morning routine: feeding my animals, taking a shower, getting dressed. I'm a writer, so I showed myself sitting down and getting some work done, but then getting bored and shooting some baskets and playing with a Lightsaber, funny stuff like that.

Then it went into a photo montage of my life, with me telling my life story over it: how I got fat, how I got skinny, how I went to college, how I did triathlons, how I got fat again.

It ends with me saying "Now that you saw my life story, let me show you who I really am. Let's go out and party!" And I put a collection of video clips of me partying hard. I really wanted to show them the character of who I would be on the show.

MR: And who was that character?

AS: I was trying to be the crazy, partying, madman jock. Not really the frat guy, but the crazy jock who's too cool for the frat guys. I wanted to show that I have tons of friends, I can get along with anyone, I'm a lot of fun, and I just happen to be a little overweight. But it's not, like, a big issue—I'd just rather be skinny. I wanted them to see that I have a great life, even though I've been struggling with this weight issue since I was a kid.

You've got to make the people who are watching your tape feel something for you. Like I know in Gary's [another contestant on *The Biggest Loser*] tape, he talked about his family and how he was scared he wouldn't be around long because of his weight. And Kelly Mac [another contestant on *The Biggest Loser*, and a comedian] talked about how, no matter how funny she was, in the back of her mind she always felt sad because of her weight. You've got to hone in on some kind of emotion.

When I decided to really go for the show, I made it impossible for them to say no. I had to make them feel like I was a sure thing. The only problem was, they thought I was too skinny for the show. So in the video, I really had to talk them into the idea of me as a fat person. My whole video was purposely made to show myself in an unflattering light. I only used pictures of me that made me look fat. I talked a lot about how I grew up fat, how my family was fat, how I had struggled with it my whole life. I wanted them to think that I was a fat guy, but at the same time really fun. The funny fat guy—that's what I was going for.

I knew everyone else was going to be going for the "I've-had-such-a-hard-life-because-I'm-fat" thing. I also knew they couldn't have a whole show based on sad, fat people—therefore I was going to be the fun one who would help the show not get too depressing.

I think that's why, when I got to the house, I realized I was the only one who didn't *have* to be there and, in the end, that's why I got kicked off—because they all felt I didn't need to be there as much as everyone else. They knew I'd be fine if I left.

MR: What happened after you finished your video?

AS: I was going to mail it in, but I had been working so hard on it—editing it and getting it ready—that I realized I had let the deadline get too close. I was worried if I mailed it in it would show up late, so I hand-delivered it instead.

I just showed up at the front gate at NBC on the day of the deadline. They kept me waiting there a long time because, of course, I didn't have an appointment or anything. I was worried they wouldn't even remember who I was. Finally they let me in, and I went right up into their offices.

Sure enough, standing right in the lobby is the cute hot chick: Alison Kass, the casting coordinator. She sees me and does this quick double-take, turns around, and says "Hey, you're Aaron, right?" I was so happy that she knew who I was. Honestly, I didn't even care about the show—I was like, "This hot chick wants me!"

I handed her my video and said "You should go put it in right now because it's hilarious." Then I turned around and left. That was it.

About four days later they called me, and all they said was, "Don't lose any more weight." I was like, "Does that mean I'm on the show?" And they said "I'll just tell you this: Legally, I can't tell you to put on weight. But do me a favor and don't skip any meals."

From that point on, they called me about once a week—never telling me if I was on the show or not, but just asking me to fill out different forms, asking me for papers from my doctor, things like that.

As it got closer to finals, they told me things like, "We pitched you yesterday, the networks love you, you don't have to worry about anything." Alison Kass sent me E-mails saying that she was the one that put me on the show, even though she couldn't tell me "yes" or "no" officially. Everyone was telling me not to worry about it.

After that, they took me to finals and sequestered me in a hotel in L.A. Sixteen of us made it to finals, and only twelve made it to the show, but I wasn't allowed to see any of them until the first day of the show.

It was crazy. There were times when they took us to the doctor, and there would be nine of us in a van and we all had to be blindfolded with these adult blindfolds that were probably bought at a cheap porn store. It was funny.

The day we went to the ranch [the setting for the show], they had all of us in a van, blindfolded, not allowed to talk to each other for three whole hours. When we got there, they pulled over to the side of the road, got us out of the van, and told us to take off our blindfolds. That was the first time we saw each other.

MR: What was your strategy for getting on *The Biggest Loser*?

AS: My first strategy was to make a video they couldn't say no to. I thought to myself, "If I was stuck in a production company office all day watching these videos, what would I want to see? I'd want to see movie parodies—a story with a beginning, a middle, and a high-powered ending that was unforgettable."

For the interview, I went in with a more mellow vibe. I didn't want to have a hyper, "Put-me-on-your-show!" energy. I figured the more subtle I was, the better—but at the same time I had to stand out. I worked really hard to come up with answers that were really funny. I was telling them stories from my childhood and acting them out for them, acting excited some times and calm and laid-back others. I wanted to show them all my sides.

Even when I was told I wasn't fat enough for the show, I wasn't worried. I just got the feeling that everyone—from Alison Kass to the guy who interviewed me—all wanted me for the show.

MR: What advice would you give someone who wanted to be on *The Biggest Loser*?

AS: You have to have an emotional grasp of who you are. You also have to have an idea of what type of story you want to tell—not just to the producers, but to America.

In my video, I kept saying "I am America. Don't call me too skinny. Most of America is forty pounds overweight. They're not all obese—they're like me. I am relatable and I'm what America wants to watch."

When they took me to take my psych test before getting on the show, the psychologist said to me "I'm going to give you the secret of reality TV: Make your own story—because if you don't, they'll edit one for you." Basically, you have to give them a story that shows you have an agenda. My agenda was, "I'm going to show Americans how they can lose weight and have fun, because I know how to do it, I've done it before, and I'll do it again." If you can make them think you're as marketable as that, you'll get on.

MR: Would you do the show again?

AS: I don't think I'd do another reality show. Being on reality TV is not fun. There's so many days when you're there and it just doesn't make sense to you. They create the reality that you live in. It can be very frustrating. The only thing that's real on reality TV are your reactions. But I love being under 200 pounds and feeling the way I feel. I wouldn't trade that for anything.

Aaron Semel lives in Los Angeles, CA, with Angel, his iguana, and Left Ear Lopez, his bunny. He is a writer of screenplays and novels.

COLD TURKEY

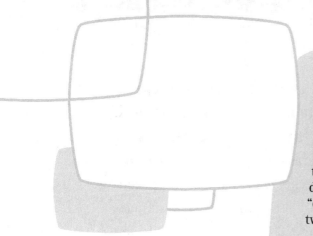

STAT SHEET

PREMISE:
Ten unsuspecting chain smokers, who all think they've been cast on their dream reality show, discover that their actual task is to quit smoking "cold turkey" while sequestered in a house for twenty-four days.

HOST:
A. J. Benza

NETWORK:
PAX

YEARS RUNNING:
Season 1 first aired in October of 2004.

CONTACT:
PAX—Phone: (888) 467-2988
Web: *www.paxtv.com/shows/coldturk/*

PRODUCTION COMPANY:
Krasnow Productions

EXECUTIVE PRODUCERS:
Stuart Krasnow, Murray Valeriano,
Jeremy Wallace

CONTESTANT AGE RANGE:
21 and up

NUMBER OF APPLICANTS PER SEASON:
5,000

NUMBER OF CONTESTANTS CHOSEN:
Ten

Since the premise of *Cold Turkey* is that chain smokers are duped into locking themselves in a house with no cigarettes for three weeks, it's a bit hard to advertise directly for the show. In fact, each season will become more difficult to cast—because as people become more familiar with the show, they'll start getting more and more suspicious during the casting process. Regardless, I'll tell you how the casting process worked during the first season, and hopefully it will help you get on the show. And if you don't make it onto the show, you should quit smoking anyway. It's bad for you. Like, *super*-bad.

The Audition Process

Most of the casting for the show's first season was conducted by street recruiters or through the casting directors' personal connections. On shows like *Cold Turkey*—that is, shows appearing on smaller networks such as PAX—casting directors often "put out their feelers," asking friends and colleagues to recommend people they think would be good for the show. Since the only *real* requirement for appearing on *Cold Turkey* is a serious smoking habit, it wasn't difficult to find people who fit the bill. In addition to using word of mouth, the casting director contacted a number of applicants through community Web sites such as Friendster (*www.friendster.com*) and MySpace (*www.myspace.com*).

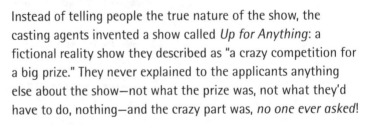

Instead of telling people the true nature of the show, the casting agents invented a show called *Up for Anything*: a fictional reality show they described as "a crazy competition for a big prize." They never explained to the applicants anything else about the show—not what the prize was, not what they'd have to do, nothing—and the crazy part was, *no one ever asked*!

WHAT THEY'RE LOOKING FOR

First off, you gotta be a chain smoker. I'm not talking about a social smoker—I'm talking about the kind of smoker who has to have a cigarette first thing in the morning with coffee. A real-deal smoker, yellow teeth and all.

Aside from that, the icing on the cake is a good personality. The casting team wants someone who can hold their interest and who speaks well—the basic stuff. Being super-hot is not a prerequisite; the producers are more concerned with the contestants' personalities.

The casting team also likes diversity. They cast Carol—a sixty-two-year-old smoker who had been smoking for forty years and whose daughter wanted her to quit—but they also cast Francesca-a crazy, punk-rock, Kelly Osborne-type who throws fits all the time, and who said of herself, "I'm a Jewish princess. I'm not gonna let anyone tell me what to do." The bottom line: They're looking for all kinds of people.

But remember: This isn't a show that casts publicly, so you're gonna have to get lucky with this one. But do me a favor: Don't start smoking just to get on the show. I can't have that kind of guilt on my shoulders.

Not even in the final stages of casting! In fact, the casting director told me that the only thing about which applicants seemed concerned was whether they would have to "eat anything gross." One applicant quit his job, and another postponed college for an entire semester—just to be on *Up for Anything*, a show they knew virtually nothing about! Oh, reality TV, we love you.

If you've seen the first episode of Season 1, you know how angry the contestants were when they found out why they were *really* there. But the casting director told me that the situation was much scarier off-camera. Contestants were screaming for the casting director, shouting things like, "She totally lied to me!"; "If I ever see her again . . . "; and every expletive in the book. Eventually, once people realized that most of them were there because they had loved ones who were worried about their health, they got used to the idea.

But is this legal? You betcha. When you sign up for a reality TV show, you sign your life away. The producers can lie to you, put you into dangerous situations, ruin your life—pretty much whatever they want. I gotta get me one of them shows.

Did You Know?

More than 400,000 Americans die each year from tobacco-related disease. In fact, someone dies from a smoking-related disease every seventy-two seconds in this country! Smoking causes more death than alcohol, illegal drugs, AIDS, car crashes, fires, murders, and suicides combined. You get it? *It's bad for you.*

FEAR FACTOR

STAT SHEET

PREMISE:
Contestants' greatest fears become reality as they face three terrifying stunts in a competition to win $50,000.

HOST:
Joe Rogan

NETWORK:
NBC

YEARS RUNNING:
The first episode aired in June of 2001.

CONTACT:
Web: *www.nbc.com/Fear_Factor*

PRODUCTION COMPANY:
Endemol Productions

EXECUTIVE PRODUCERS:
John De Mol, Matt Kunitz

CONTESTANT AGE RANGE:
21 and up

NUMBER OF APPLICANTS PER SEASON:
30,000

NUMBER OF CONTESTANTS CHOSEN:
Eight per episode, 8–33 episodes per season

If an average Tuesday for you consists of climbing atop a car while it's dangling from a building, eating twenty live Madagascar Hissing Beetles, and freeing yourself from handcuffs while repeatedly being dunked underwater, then *Fear Factor* wants nothing to do with you.

However, if the thought of these stunts scares the bejesus out of you—but at the same time makes you think "Hmmm, I guess I could do that for $50,000 bucks!"—then step right up to the freakiest of reality-TV freak shows. You and *Fear Factor* are a match made in heaven.

The Audition Process

There are two ways to get on *Fear Factor*: open calls and video applications. The nice thing about the show's casting department is that, for the most part, it casts year-round and accepts video applications 365 days a year.

But first things first. Visit *www.nbc.com/Fear_Factor* for the most up-to-date casting information and any possible changes they've made to the audition process. Also, the show often holds casting calls for specific types of contestants—for example, honeymooners, models, wrestlers, etc.—so check the Web site to see whether you fit the bill.

Open Calls

Fear Factor open calls are usually advertised on morning radio programs, often while Joe Rogan himself is appearing as a guest, or on NBC local affiliates, usually following a *Fear Factor* episode. In keeping with the young-and-beautiful vibe of the show, most open calls are held at clubs or bars.

You'll be asked to bring a recent photo of yourself and to show up early, as the show draws a huge number of applicants at each open call. If you're able to bring two photos of yourself, a close-up and a full-body shot, the casting department will think you're sexy—or at least well-prepared.

At the call, you'll be asked to complete a short six- to ten-page application asking for general information and a few interesting tidbits about yourself. Then you'll be seated at a table for your audition.

Fear Factor uses the group interview method, seating twelve people at a table and having a moderator (casting associate) pose questions in the hopes of sparking interesting conversation. Since the show caters to very competitive types, the casting associates like to stir things up a bit at these open calls—often pitting wannabe contestants against each other in verbal showdowns. Expect questions like: "Who do you think you could easily beat at this table in a challenge involving physical strength?" Ideally for the casting team, this question would cause a big muscle guy to point to a skinny guy in glasses and yell "That guy! He's a wimp!"—thus baiting the skinny guy in glasses to stand up and shout "No way, man! I'm fast and wily. I could take you down!" Muscle guy would then grunt and shake his fist in the air. Skinny guy would grit his teeth and scowl. End scene.

While these interactions ideally don't end up in fisticuffs, the casting team still wants to see you duke it out a bit—verbally. The point of the exercise is to separate the energetic, confident—dare I say?—*loud-mouthed* applicants from the shy wallflowers who might clam up in front of the camera. While the casting team isn't just looking for a bunch of bullies to cast on its show, it does want to see people who aren't afraid to do whatever it takes—like making a fool of yourself at an open call—to get on *Fear Factor* and win the money.

While researching this book, I met a woman named Michelle who was cast on *Fear Factor* after attending an open call in New Jersey. She explained to me that, for the majority of her ten-minute group interview, she didn't say a word. Then, right at the end, she stopped the conversation and listed the weaknesses and flaws of each potential applicant at the table, taking them out one by one. She played the role of the calm, cool, and collected competitor, and it worked. The casting people were impressed by her, and she ended up being the only one at her table asked to stick around to fill out a long application.

The long application clocks in at around sixty pages and takes close to an hour to complete. Expect essay questions about your aspirations, personal life, and, most important, your fears. Once you've completed the application, it's time to go home and wait by the phone.

Video Application

If you can't make it to an open call near you, then a video application is your best bet. The casting team is looking for a five-minute videotape of you, in plain view and with clear sound, explaining why you would make an excellent candidate for *Fear Factor*.

Start off with your name and hometown, and then jump right into a description of your best attributes: what makes you a fierce competitor, what you're most afraid of, and a few big obstacles you've overcome in your life. Do not—I repeat, do not—attempt any stunts on your tape. The casting directors don't want to see you eat a worm from your garden. They don't want to see you jump over your car on a skateboard. In fact, because the producers don't want to encourage participation in dangerous and unsupervised stunts, anyone performing a stunt in his or her video application will automatically be disqualified.

Be entertaining, be real, and be confident. Also, just because you *can* talk for five whole minutes doesn't mean you have to. Don't sit there staring at the camera after three and a half minutes because you want to kill time. If you're bored in your interview, trust me: the casting department is twice as bored. At the end

SEND YOUR TAPE TO:

★ ★

Last but not least, you'll need two recent photos of yourself: one close-up and one full-body. Put them in a package with your VHS tape and filled-out application, and send the whole thing to:

★ ★

Fear Factor Casting—[City Name]
1149 N. Gower, Suite 105
Los Angeles, CA 90038

★ ★

For your "City Name," pick the city from the following list that is closest to where you live. This is the city to which you'll be expected to travel, at your own expense, should you advance to Round Two.

1. Seattle, WA
2. Portland, OR
3. San Francisco, CA
4. Los Angeles, CA
5. Phoenix, AZ
6. Denver, CO
7. Minneapolis, MN
8. Cleveland, OH
9. Chicago, IL
10. Austin, TX
11. Memphis, TN
12. Boston, MA
13. New York, NY
14. Philadelphia, PA
15. Washington, DC
16. Atlanta, GA
17. Miami, FL
18. Honolulu, HI

of your self-interview, they recommend zooming out with your camera so they can get a full look at your body.

Fear Factor accepts only VHS tapes, so if you're shooting on a home video camera that outputs onto Hi8 or Mini-DV, make sure you plug your camera into your VCR when you're done and record your video application onto a VHS tape. Label your tape with your name, age, address, and phone number.

Visit *www.nbc.com/Fear_Factor* to download the application—click on the "Apply" button, and then the "Download Application" button. The application asks for fairly basic information: your name, age, occupation, and a checklist of possible fears to help the casting department get a better idea of what stunts would freak you out the most should you be cast on the show. Some of the more bizarre options on the list? Lakes, The Boogie Man, and Cooties. Hmmm, I can't remember the last time they had a cootie-related stunt on *Fear Factor*. . . .

A Special Note for Couples, Families, Twins, and Siblings

Fear Factor is looking for you as well! The show is always accepting applications for couples, families, twins, and siblings. So get out those cameras and get to work! Here's the rules:

Only one videotape will be accepted per group, and the length of your tape cannot exceed five minutes. Include a group interview on your tape, as well as an interview with each individual. Each person must fill out his or her own separate application and supply two recent photos, a close-up and a full-body shot. So, for example, if you're applying as twins, your package should contain one videotape, two applications, and four photos.

Be sure to indicate "couple," "family," "twins," or "siblings" in big letters next to the mailing address on your package. Good luck!

Round Two and Beyond

Whether you applied with a video application or at an open call, Round Two will consist of a taped interview with a few members of the casting team somewhere in a city near you. Prior to your thirty-minute interview you'll receive a long, sixty-page application (if you weren't given one at an open call). The majority of your thirty-minute interview will be spent talking about the answers you give on this application, so make sure your answers are interesting and entertaining and, most important, make sure you choose topics you feel comfortable talking about in front of a camera.

If your interview goes well, you'll be flown to Los Angeles to undergo medical and psychological testing, and to conduct interviews with the show's producers and a few network executives. If you continue to demonstrate that you'd be an entertaining contestant on the show, you'll be cast—and you'll have the opportunity to prove to the world that fear is not a factor for you.

WHAT THEY'RE LOOKING FOR

Fear Factor is looking for outgoing, attractive, young people who aren't afraid of a camera, but who are afraid of lots of other things. The casting department wants you to be scared to perform the show's stunts, but not so scared that you won't go through with them.

In addition, the casting team likes to cast a certain number of contestants who will fill certain "roles" on the show—for example, the trash-talker, the nice guy, the bimbo, or the brains. If you think you naturally fit one of these roles, all the better for you. It's best not to fake it, however; casting directors tend to easily detect when applicants are pretending to be someone they're not.

Finally, you must be in tip-top condition and brimming with confidence to withstand the physical and mental challenges that will be thrown at you during the three days of filming. Also, it helps if you have a strong stomach—a really, really strong stomach. Go get 'em!

Did You Know?

One of my all-time favorite reality-TV stories, which I heard while researching this book, involves a woman who went through the entire casting process for *Fear Factor*, went to an open call, filled out the applications, drove a hundred miles to do her Round Two interview, met with the producers, and actually got cast on the show—only to call the producers and tell them she changed her mind and didn't want to be on the show anymore. Why, you ask? Because she was too scared to fly to Los Angeles. I love it!

Did You Know?

Fear Factor is actually based on a Dutch reality TV show called *Now or Neverland*, which is almost exactly like *Fear Factor* but has a considerably smaller budget.

THE
REBEL BILLIONAIRE:
BRANSON'S QUEST
FOR THE BEST

STAT SHEET

PREMISE:
Sir Richard Branson, the colorful founder and chairman of the Virgin Group of companies, will whisk away sixteen of America's best and brightest on the adventure of a lifetime. The one person who can keep up with him the longest will win a mind-blowing prize.

HOST:
Richard Branson

NETWORK:
FOX

YEARS RUNNING:
Season 1 first aired in November of 2004.

CONTACT:
Bunim/Murray–Phone: (818) 754-5790
Web: *www.bunim-murray.com*

PRODUCTION COMPANY:
Bunim/Murray

EXECUTIVE PRODUCERS:
Richard Branson, Jonathan Murray,
Lori Levin-Hyams, Laura Fuest, Tod Dahlke,
Kevin Lee, John Gypton

CONTESTANT AGE RANGE:
18 and up

NUMBER OF APPLICANTS PER SEASON:
10,000

NUMBER OF CONTESTANTS CHOSEN:
Sixteen

What happens when you take two cups of *The Apprentice*, a dollop of *Fear Factor*, a pinch of *The Amazing Race*, a few drops of rock n' roll attitude and mix it all up in a big bowl? Well, I think you get my Nana's recipe for potato pancakes, but you *also* get *The Rebel Billionaire: Branson's Quest for the Best*. Whether you're looking for a leg up in the business world, a chance to travel all over the world, or just want to try high tea atop a hot air balloon floating ten thousand feet in the sky, then look no further than this show.

The Audition Process

Since this is a Bumin/Murray show, its casting process is almost identical to the the one used for *The Real World*, with a few exceptions.

It all begins by either mailing in a video or attending an open casting call.

Open Casting Calls

The best way to find out about open casting calls for *The Rebel Billionaire* is to regularly check FOX's Web site (*www.fox.com*) or stay tuned to local FOX affiliates, which will advertise casting calls happening in your area. Another great place to check is your local Virgin Megastore—since Richard Branson owns Virgin, open calls often take place at Megastores all over the country.

Once you're standing in line at an open call, a casting associate will snap your Polaroid and hand you a short application to fill out. Eventually you'll be seated at a table with ten other people who were waiting in line with you. A casting associate will do his or her best to spark conversation amongst the group, mostly by asking pointed and/or controversial questions. And because of the show's business theme, expect questions about hot-button issues that are also business-related—for example, "How do you feel about affirmative action in the workplace?" or "In what hiring situations do you think employers should be allowed to discriminate against homosexuals?"

After ten minutes, the casting team will send you on your way. But if they liked your group interview, they'll send someone to discreetly tap you on the shoulder and ask you to stick around for a bit.

Then you'll be asked to fill out an extended application, usually around sixteen pages long. Be prepared to give long-winded answers—the more information the better. Completing the application should take you an hour to an hour and a half. A quick tip: Make sure you do your best to spell correctly and write everything legibly. On a show like *The Rebel Billionaire*, where the casting team is looking for the brightest young Americans they can find, the fastest way to blow your chances is to make your application look like it was written by a four-year-old. This may seem obvious, but the casting directors tell me it's almost shocking how many people, all of whom seemed like promising candidates in person, have submitted applications that look like they completed them while drunk.

If the casting department likes your application, you'll get a call pretty quickly asking you to come back in a few days for an hour-long camera interview.

Video Application

For a detailed set of tips on completing your video application, see the "Video Application" section of *The Real World* chapter in this book. Because of *The Rebel Billionaire*'s business theme, however, I also recommend that you use the video to highlight your competitive nature and entrepreneurial drive. Talk about your business experiences and your goals for the future. The casting team isn't *just* looking for great personalities—it also wants fierce competitors with drive. And remember: This isn't *The Apprentice*. Instead of sitting in a boardroom, you're gonna be jumping out of planes and bungee jumping into crocodile-infested waters. So make sure your video lets the casting team know that you're as committed to the adventure elements of the show as you are to the business elements.

Round Two and Beyond

Generally, 75 percent of applicants are asked to come back for a camera interview. And get ready, because these interviews can be intense. A well-facilitated Bunim/Murray interview should lead you through a series of emotions: sadness, happiness, and anger. Before the casting associate will let the interview come to end, he or she will make sure you've taken a full turn on the emotional rollercoaster: laughing, crying, screaming with rage—the whole nine yards. Much like good FBI interrogators, the casting directors know what it takes to elicit emotional responses from applicants, so don't be afraid to go there. Let them guide you. And if you're not the kind of person who feels comfortable expressing his or her emotions in front of a camera or a bunch of strangers, then *The Rebel Billionaire* (and most of reality TV) is not for you.

The hour-long interview will focus on three main topics: family, career, and future goals, with about twenty minutes dedicated to each topic. They'll lead you through some of the more painful stories of your life, asking you to elaborate on certain sections. They'll ask you what you're afraid of and how you would react if forced to face those fears. They'll also expect you to laugh and show your lighter side as well. Be prepared to cry, laugh, and get angry at least once while in your interview.

Also, make sure you give *long* answers to the interview questions. The fastest way to elicit a "Don't call us, we'll call you" is to provide two-word answers to the interviewers' questions. Casting directors often describe someone who performs well during a camera interview as having "popped" on-camera. "Popping" basically means staying yourself and having no problem opening up to the camera—possibly even less trouble than you had participating in your roundtable discussion during Round One. "Popping" makes you memorable. "Popping" is your goal.

Once your interview is over, the casting team will review your entire packet, which consists of your long application, your short application, your Polaroid photo, and an edited version of your hour-long camera interview. Working together, they'll pare down the remaining contenders to a group of forty or fifty finalists. Those finalists will be flown to Los Angeles and subjected to the usual barrage of health

WHEN YOUR TAPE IS READY, SEND IT OFF TO:

★★★★★★★★★★★★★★★★★★★★★★

The Rebel Billionaire Casting
Bunim/Murray Productions
6007 Sepulveda Blvd
Van Nuys, CA 91411

★★★★★★★★★★★★★★★★★★★★★★

WHAT THEY'RE LOOKING FOR

The first season of *The Rebel Billionaire* was pitched on the radio to would-be auditioners as "The new version of *The Apprentice*. . . but nobody's going to be selling lemonade on this show—they'll be jumping out of planes instead!" This should give you a good idea of what the casting team looks for in an ideal cast member.

They want the best and brightest of the business world, but they also want adventurers—people who aren't afraid to try new things, to push themselves to the limit, and to prove to Richard Branson just how dedicated they are to being the best. As you might expect, the differences between contestants on *The Apprentice* and contestants on *The Rebel Billionaire* are similar to the differences between Donald Trump and Richard Branson. Branson is a bit wilder, a bit more "rock 'n' roll," and so is his show. Keep this in mind during all stages of the auditioning process.

Another way in which *The Rebel Billionaire* differs from *The Apprentice* is that, in order to become a contestant on *The Rebel Billionaire*, you don't already have to be successful in the business world. *The Rebel Billionaire*'s Season 1 cast was peopled not just with business leaders and entrepreneurs, but also with a model, a pro tennis player, and a used-car salesman. The casting team is as interested in your leadership *potential* as it is in your leadership *experience*.

Finally, the casting directors told me that the main traits they look for in *Rebel Billionaire* applicants are intelligence, drive, and physical fitness. *The Rebel Billionaire* relies as much on your brawn as it does your brain—so hit the gym a bit before showing up in line at the open casting call. Good luck!

examinations, psychological evaluations, and interviews with both Bunim/Murray and FOX network executives.

The final interviews will be similar to the first hour-long camera interview, but slightly less intense. The producers want to get a feel for who you are, how you interact with others, and how you cope under stress.

After final interviews are completed, Bunim/Murray and FOX executives will pick the show's final cast.

Did You Know?

In 2004, Virgin founder and CEO Richard Branson announced plans to launch the world's first commercial space flights. Under the banner of Virgin Galactic, Branson plans to send thousands of wealthy adventurers into orbit sometime within the next five years. Tickets start at close to $200,000. That better come with at least one meal and an in-flight movie!

STREET SMARTS

Reality-TV confession #4,081: I love *Street Smarts*. Maybe it's because I love tickling my brain with obscure pop-culture trivia, or maybe it's because I love laughing at stupid people. Either way, when I can't fall asleep I just turn on *Street Smarts*, revel in a nice moment of intellectual superiority, and drift off into dreamland.

Street Smarts takes people on the street who seem to have shockingly low I.Q.s and then lets two in-studio contestants make wagers on whether they think the people on the street will get insanely easy trivia questions right or wrong. I often wonder if the people on the street are actors playing "dumb" because I really can't fathom someone not knowing what the national language of Italy is, but the casting directors swear to me that the people are genuine. Scary.

The Audition Process

There are two possible roles for contestants on *Street Smarts*: staying in the studio or getting ridiculed on the street. The people in the studio win the money. The people on the street look like morons. Why anyone would actually want to be one of the morons on the street is beyond me, but hey, they're morons! Bless their sweet, small little minds.

STAT SHEET

PREMISE:
A pop-culture reality game show in
which contestants prove how smart they are
by predicting how dumb other people can be!

HOST:
Frank Nicotero

NETWORK:
WB

YEARS RUNNING:
Debuted in October 2000

CONTACT:
Phone: (877) 564-SMART
Web: *www.streetsmartstv.com*

PRODUCTION COMPANY:
Dawn Syndicated Productions, in association
with Telepictures Productions

EXECUTIVE PRODUCER:
Scott St. John

CONTESTANT AGE RANGE:
18 and up

NUMBER OF APPLICANTS PER SEASON:
2,000

NUMBER OF CONTESTANTS CHOSEN:
Three people on the street and two people
in the studio for each episode, about twenty
episodes per season

In-Studio Contestants

To be an in-studio contestant, call the show's hotline at (877) 564-SMART and leave your name and telephone number. If you live outside of the Los Angeles area, don't bother calling—there's absolutely no shortage of people trying to get on television in L.A., so there's no way they're going to fly you into town to be on their show. If you're coming to L.A. to visit, however, that's a different story—give them a call.

The cool thing about the *Street Smarts* hotline is that *every* person who leaves a message gets called back for an audition. That means this is one show on which you really do stand a good chance of landing a spot. While it's hard to come up with a specific number for the ratio of people who call in to people who get cast, I'd say less than a hundred people audition each week, which in contrast to your average reality TV show gives you very good odds. Pay attention here, and I'll make it even easier for you.

When you come in for your audition, you'll have to fill out a long application with general information about yourself. There's only one question on this application that really matters, and here it is: "Tell us three things about yourself: something funny, something scary, and something that nobody else would know." Before you arrive for your audition, make sure you prepare three short, entertaining anecdotes as answers to this question. Make your stories as outrageously memorable as you can. And if you don't have any outrageously memorable stories from your life. . . make them up!

Once you've completed your application, you'll be placed in front of a camera and asked to repeat or expand upon one of the three short anecdotes you included in your application. Be animated, outgoing, and funny when you tell your story. Laugh out loud a few times. Be boisterous. Honestly, they're really not that picky. As long as you're cute enough for television, it should work.

If the casting directors like you, they'll call you back for a phone interview. Make sure to be just as energetic and funny on the phone as your were in your on-camera audition. The whole point of this phone call is for the casting team to try to catch you off guard—to find out if your fun-loving personality was all an act. If your phone interview goes well, you'll get cast on the show and will have the chance to win $4,000 by figuring out how stupid some people truly are.

The show doesn't cast the people on the street in advance: They simply go to crowded places and ask random people to fill out questionnaires. In one of my favorite examples of reality-TV irony, the more questions you get wrong on the questionnaire, the better the chance you have to appear on the show. The questions include: "What color is the White House?"; "What planet are you from?"; and "What day is it?" If the question "What color is the White House?" makes you scratch the side of your head for a moment before answering "Tan," then you're going to be a great addition to a *Street Smarts* episode. If you *really* want to be a street person (and I don't mean homeless) on *Street Smarts*, my casting connections tell me that, if you call the hotline and tell the casting team you're interested, they'll let you know when and where their camera crew will be showing up next. You can then hustle to where the camera crew is filming, fill out the questionnaire, and wow them with your . . . intellectual modesty.

What They're Looking For

In a nutshell:
• In-studio contestants: Energetic nutcases with common sense.
• People on the street: Energetic nutcases with no common sense.

Did You Know?

Some of my favorite *Street Smarts* episodes are the ones that feature celebrity match-ups! Some of the celebs who have made it onto the show are Gary Coleman, Todd Bridges, the cast of *Dallas*, the cast of *Gilligan's Island*, the cast of *The Love Boat*, and every Californian's favorite porn-star-who-ran-for-governor: Mary Carey!

STAT SHEET

PREMISE:
Sixteen or so average Americans are dumped in a remote and unforgiving location to find out who can survive the bugs, the rain, the hunger and—most important—the tribal councils, to become the final Survivor and win a million dollars.

HOST:
Jeff Probst

NETWORK:
CBS

YEARS RUNNING:
Season 1, *Survivor: Borneo*, debuted in May of 2000.

CONTACT:
CBS—Phone: (323) 575-2345
Web: *www.cbs.com/survivor*

CREATOR:
Mark Burnett

EXECUTIVE PRODUCER:
Mark Burnett

CONTESTANT AGE RANGE:
21 and up

NUMBER OF APPLICANTS PER SEASON:
50,000

NUMBER OF CONTESTANTS CHOSEN:
Sixteen-Twenty

SURVIVOR

Outwit. Outplay. Outlast. Outstanding! As my all-time favorite reality TV show, *Survivor* occupies a special place in my heart when it comes to casting. In my humble opinion, *Survivor* has consistently assembled the best reality-TV casts in television history.

Every season a fresh batch of future reality-TV stars are dumped into a remote location and made to fend for themselves against the elements. If having no food, water, or shelter wasn't bad enough, these 'survivors' also have to figure out how to connive and manipulate one another in order to survive the voting-off ceremony at each week's tribal council. Oh yeah, and sometimes they also have to eat rats.

If one thing can be said about reality-TV fame, it's that it is fleeting. Yet five years later, we're still talking about the most legendary contestants from *Survivor*: Richard Hatch, Rudy Boesch, Colby Donaldson, Ethan Zohn, and Boston Rob. Ah, the memories.

Getting on *Survivor* is the pinnacle of reality-TV achievement. It is the grand triumph. It is also one of the hardest darn shows to land a spot on, falling just a bit short of *American Idol*'s numbers in terms of annual auditioners.

But even though the competition is stiff, the following pages will provide you with step-by-step information on how best to wow Mark Burnett's well-trained casting department and earn yourself a buff, a torch, and a spot on next season's *Survivor*. The tribe is about to speak.

The Audition Process

Usually toward the end of every *Survivor* season, CBS will start running ads for next season's auditions. *Survivor* auditions work in the same way as the majority of CBS's reality shows: through open calls and video applications. In fact, the audition process is very similar to that of *The Amazing Race*, with a few important distinctions. Survivors ready? Read on!

Open Calls

The best way to find out about open calls is by watching your local CBS affiliate. If there is going to be an open call in your area, the affiliate will make sure that you hear about it during prime time, probably a week in advance of the actual event. Because you need to be watching at just the right time, finding out about these calls can be pretty hit-or-miss. But if you keep your eyes and ears peeled (they occasionally advertise the auditions on morning radio stations), you should be able to find out about the next call being held in your area.

It's a good idea to have your application filled out before you arrive at the open call. The application can be downloaded from the CBS Web site (*www.cbs.com/survivor*), or by visiting the Web site of your local affiliate. (It's the same application either way, so don't stress out about downloading from one site or the other.) The application is a general get-to-know-you form that asks simple, short-answer questions about your life. While your interview is a much more important part of the auditioning process, the short application can serve as a great reminder of your outgoing personality and your interesting background for a casting director who is reviewing your file.

At *Survivor* open calls, CBS implements the "cattle call" audition strategy, in which casting associates line up thousands of people and then parade them, one at a time, in front of a camera. Once you're in front of the camera, a casting associate will ask you to state your name, age, occupation, and where you're from. He or she will then give you three minutes to make a case as to why you should be on *Survivor*.

The two- to three-minute time limit is fairly strict: Even if you're in mid-sentence at the three-minute mark, the casting associate will turn off the camera and thank you for your time. To the casting department watching your tape back in Los Angeles, it doesn't look good if you're cut off in the middle of a sentence. This could easily ruin your chance to make it to the semifinals, so keep it short. In fact, it's best to have your two- to three-minute speech planned and rehearsed before you show up. My source in casting told me that these are the points the casting team wants you to hit during your speech:

★ An anecdote from your life in which you learned a valuable lesson that has made you a stronger person and/or a better competitor.

★ A strategy or mistake that you observed in a previous *Survivor* cast member or season that you think you could improve upon.

★ A reason why you think you deserve either the prize money or the experience of being a *Survivor* cast member more than anyone else.

Sounds like a lot to talk about in less than three minutes, doesn't it? But remember: You don't have to hit all these points separately. You could tell one story that encompasses two, if not all three, of these topics. Also, keep in mind that there may be a few other people to your left and right doing their interviews at the same time, so do your best not to be distracted. Pretend it's just you, the camera, and the casting department watching your tape in Los Angeles.

Once they've whisked you away from the camera and accepted your application, you're free to go. Don't be discouraged if no one runs after you to ask you to stick around for a second interview. No one gets called back the day of the open call. In fact, even if the casting team likes you, you won't hear from them for at least a few weeks.

Video Application

If you're planning to submit a video application, the first thing you should do is visit *www.cbs.com/survivor*. If the show is casting, the Web site will provide all the information you need to create your video, as well as a PDF version (an Adobe Acrobat file) of the ten-page application.

The video should be no longer than three minutes, and should be recorded on either a mini-DV or VHS tape. The majority of the taped self-interview should consist of you, shot from the shoulders up, speaking clearly and looking directly at the camera. Tell the camera a bit about yourself and why you deserve to be on *Survivor*. (Since the casting directors are looking for the same content whether you apply by video or at an open casting call, see the "Open Calls" section of this chapter for additional information about what to include in your video.)

Again, the casting department is very strict about the maximum length of your tape, so don't even think about talking past the three-minute mark. If you do, no one will watch it.

Once you've sent off your application, cross your fingers and hope for the best!

Round Two and Beyond

Approximately eight hundred people get called back for Round Two, also known as the semifinals. The semifinalists, divided (usually unevenly) amongst the thirteen regions, will be asked to come to their selected cities for a long interview lasting twenty to thirty minutes. Note that this trip will *not* be financed by CBS, so you'll have to pay for your own transportation, accommodations, and food during the semifinals. But the good news is that you'll have only one interview, so if you live near your selected city, you should be able to drive there and back again on the same day, making gas your only expense.

If you get a call inviting you to a Round Two interview, CBS will send you an extended application, about sixty pages long. This application consists of essay questions that will require you to discuss your life at length. When you come in for your long interview, you will be asked to discuss in person many of the answers you provided on your application, so think hard about what you write. Make sure you provide answers you'll feel comfortable talking about in front of a camera, and that will be entertaining for the casting team to hear. Many people make the mistake of providing answers on the written application that they're embarrassed to discuss in public. This will make you look nervous and "spacey" in your long interview; don't do it.

A good way to practice for your long interview is to conduct a "mock" interview: Have a friend ask you the questions on your long application, and answer back as if you were speaking to a casting director or camera.

Not all second-round interviews last a full thirty minutes. But while a twenty-minute interview doesn't necessarily mean the casting team didn't like you, a five-minute interview is almost always a bad sign. The

SEND YOUR TAPE TO:

★★★★★★★★★★★★★★★★★★★★★★★

Once your tape is done, attach your application along with proof of citizenship (a photocopy of your passport or driver's license will work) and a passport-size photo (cut yourself out of a picture you already have, or head down to an amusement park and find a photo booth) and send it off to:

★★★★★★★★★★★★★★★★★★★★★★★

Survivor [City #]
2801 Ocean Park Blvd
Santa Monica, CA 90405

★★★★★★★★★★★★★★★★★★★★★★★

From the following list, pick the number that corresponds to the city closest to you and include this "city number" in the mailing address on your package. The city you select will be the city to which you will travel (at your own expense) if you are selected for the next round of auditions. (Note that the numbered cities are different from those used for Amazing Race *applications, so be sure to check your city number carefully.)*

1. Seattle, WA
2. Los Angeles, CA
3. Chicago, IL
4. Portland, ME
5. Boston, MA
6. New York, NY
7. Dallas, TX

8. Orlando, FL
9. Kansas City, KS
10. Greenville, NC/SC
11. Madison, WI
12. Pheonix, AZ

best way to keep a long interview from being cut short is to stay animated, relaxed, and personable. Remember, if the casting director feels comfortable talking to you and is enjoying the conversation, he or she is not going to turn the camera off and ask you to leave. So do your best to have fun!

Next, the group of eight hundred semifinalists will be pared down to a group of forty-eight finalists, all of whom are flown to Los Angeles, put up in a hotel (all at CBS's expense), and required to jump through a series of hoops—including medical testing, psychological testing, and a slew of interviews with casting directors, producers, and the occasional network executive. The finals can last up to ten days, during which time you'll be sequestered in your hotel room and prohibited from socializing with any other potential cast members—the producers don't want any alliances to form prior to the game.

Finally, the casting team selects sixteen cast members, who are made to sign what has to be the world's longest confidentiality report before being sent home to pack for their upcoming adventure.

Did You Know?

- For longtime host Jeff Probst, the ninth season of *Survivor*, titled *Survivor: Vanuatu*, proved to be a very special one indeed. Probst began dating Julie Berry, a survivor eliminated late in the game, after the show had finished taping. Both claimed to be very much in love. "I'm in love. I'm with her. I'm with her family, and there ain't no turning back," the 43-year-old Probst told *People* magazine. But although the couple swears their romance began only *after* the cameras stopped rolling, many *Survivor* fans were commenting on their on-camera flirtations long before their love story ever became public knowledge.

- The first episode of *Survivor: Outback* (Season Two) was aired immediately following the Super Bowl, attracting more than 50 million viewers—an all-time record for a reality TV show.

WHAT THEY'RE LOOKING FOR

What makes *Survivor* so great is the wide variety of contestants it showcases each season. The casting department likes to select a true assortment of energetic, able-bodied Americans— from young college grads to sixty-year-old truck drivers and everyone in between.

Because so many different types of contestants have proven successful in previous seasons, *Survivor* has no "perfect" candidate. The party line regarding the ideal candidate comes from the show's application, which states that *Survivor* wants contestants who are strong-willed, outgoing, adventurous, physically and mentally adept, and adaptable to new environments, and who have interesting lifestyles, backgrounds, and personalities. But the best advice I received came from a member of the show's casting department, who advised applicants to "shock us. Give us something we've never seen before. Be energetic and big and willing to do anything to win."

I recently watched the audition tapes of all the people cast on *Survivor: Vanuatu* and noticed that the majority of the applicants did one of two things: they either sat in one place and talked, very intimately, about their lives or they went outside and took the camera on a tour of their lives. The people who opted for the quiet, intimate interview were the more subdued, serious people cast on the show. Those who took the camera on a tour of their lives were the more up-beat, energetic members of the cast. Decide for yourself if you're the energetic/loud type or the quiet/serious type and make sure your video reflects your personality.

To win the million bucks, it's going to demand as much from you mentally as it will physically. To put it bluntly, *Survivor* is no joke. It's grueling and painful and long. So show the casting team that you can handle anything—that you're ready for an adventure and that you've got what it takes to go all the way to the end. If you can do that, and entertain them at the same time, you'll fare well in the casting process. The tribe has spoken.

Interview
Mitchell Olson, *Survivor: Australia*

MR: How did you get involved with *Survivor*?

    MO: I was taking commercial classes in New York City, learning how to be on commercials, and one of the gals who was in the class with me worked for NBC. At that time I was about to appear on *Wheel of Fortune*, and I brought in the whole class to watch it with me. I had also been on *The Price is Right*.

MR: So you already had a good understanding of how to get cast on a television show?

    MO: Right. And the girl who worked at NBC was like, "Since you're so into game shows, you should check out this new show I hear CBS is doing." I guess because she worked at NBC she kind of had all the dirt on the new hot shows the other networks were working on.

So I went to the Web site, read about the show, and thought it looked completely insane—but also interesting. I filled out the application, I made a video, and I sent it in, like, a week later. Here's the catch, though: that was for *Survivor* Season 1.

You see, they had a rule at the time that said no applicant could have appeared on a game show within ten years of applying to *Survivor*. This was back when *Survivor* was considered a game show and not a reality show. Since then, things have changed and reality is its own genre, so that wouldn't be an issue today. But they had a real problem with me being on all these other game shows.

MR: So did you audition again the next year?

    MO: I hadn't even planned to audition for Season 2, but the casting director called me out of the blue and said "We're sorry about the whole problem with Season 1, but we'd like you to re-audition for Season 2." So I went in and met with the exact same people and applied all over again, but this time I didn't have to make another video. Instead I came in for an interview and performed a song parody for them.

MR: What inspired you to do that?

MO: I knew they were going to bring it back to Mark Burnett, and I wanted to showcase that I was a singer/songwriter. I sang a song about Season 1 and all the hilarities with Richard Hatch. It was set to the tune of "Under the Sea," and the lyrics were about the awful things that had happened on and off the show. . . all sorts of awful things that just happened to rhyme and fit together into a funny song. The casting people had a great time with the song. They loved it.

After the song, they asked me all the usual Reality-type questions about my family, love life, if I'd be able to hack it and live with spiders and snakes, what kind of role I think I'd play stuck in the middle of nowhere, questions about alliances—all the sort of Reality questions that come up in these interviews.

I think the best piece of advice I got from someone before I went in for that interview was to "be 100 percent yourself, because if you don't get accepted and you lied about who you were, you'll really kick yourself."

From my experience as a casting director, I know that what they're looking out for is a liar. If you sense that someone is being dishonest with you and is not really who they claim to be, it's like the most obvious "We're-done-with-you" scenario. If you're trying to be Richard Hatch but you're not really Richard Hatch, then going in and trying to keep track of your lies is going to be tough, and eventually the casting people are going to catch you on it.

When I went to Los Angeles for the final interviews, Mark Burnett would drill me with the same questions day-in and day-out. I was like, "I answered these questions yesterday." And one of the casting directors had to say to me, "Just keep answering them the way you did. It's like an interrogation. He's trying to catch you in a lie so he can see if you really are who you say you are."

MR: Why do you think you made it onto *Survivor*?

> MO: I remember when I went to the finals in Los Angeles, everything went great. They narrowed it down to the top twenty, and we went to meet with Les Moonves, who was going to help make the final selection. He said to me, "What's a bad day like for you? What types of people do you hate?" And I said, "To be completely honest with you, I don't really have bad days. I don't hate certain types. I tend to get along with everyone. And I apologize if you're looking for someone more controversial, but I don't think I'm going to be able to play that card." And he stopped me mid-sentence and said "We already have our bitches and our people to do that type of stuff. We're looking for the opposite of that. So congratulations, and thank you for being honest."

> I think he appreciated that I was being straightforward. I'm sure they had a million people who were like, "If somebody does me wrong, I'm going to scream at them and go crazy." Everyone assumes reality TV means drama, and that you have to be as dramatic and evil as possible. But on my season, we all really got along and loved each other.

MR: How do you feel about how you were portrayed on the show?

> MO: I hated how I came off, but that's how most people feel. The editing isn't exactly how you experienced it. We actually had quite a bit of fun. I know part of the reason they cast me was because of the comedy I was going to bring to the table. We laughed every night, we had campfire sing-alongs—but all those things got quickly edited out. I guess it's because it's not as dramatic—it doesn't show us being stressed out and starving. If you're going to be on a reality TV show and you want to have fun, don't be disappointed if they don't air it.

MR: Do you look back on the experience fondly?

> MO: Yeah, mainly because of the friendships that I made. There's tons of benefits that us Reality people go to each year, and we look forward to them because we know we're going to see each other. It's funny to have all these people from *Big Brother*, *The Bachelor*, and *Average Joe* all hanging out in one place and having fun. We have a lot in common

with each other because not many people have gone through something like that.

MR: What advice would you give to someone who wanted to be on *Survivor* today?

MO: I think that most people fall prey to clichés in their audition videos. Like, you'll see people who sing "I Will Survive" or "I'm a Survivor" and, from what I've heard, doing that is the fastest ticket to getting your tape switched off.

The more Reality gets oversaturated, the less creative people seem to be and the more they just want to pigeonhole themselves as a certain character. If you can be extremely creative and still be yourself, then that's your best ticket onto a reality show. Also, if the show calls for an audition tape, then the first ten seconds are obviously the most crucial.

Everyone has this idea of what casting directors are looking for—like, "Oh my god, they need an Omarosa." As a casting director, I can't tell you how many times people will walk in and say things like, "I'm going to be extremely dramatic. People will want to watch your show just for me. I'm going to be such a jerk." They think I'm going to be impressed by that, but casting directors are looking for the *new* Reality character; they're not looking for copies.

Omarosa didn't walk in there thinking she was a bitch. Those are always the best people, because when you interview them, they leave thinking they're the sweetest, coolest people ever, and then two seconds later the casting directors turn to each other and say "What a bitch." Then we cast them.

Oddly enough, Mitchell now works behind the scenes of reality TV, casting for a number of big shows. When he's not busy with that, he can be found performing stand-up comedy in New York City and hosting scavenger hunts through Watson Adventures. In addition, Mitchell is currently writing two books and is a judge for the Miss America pageant.

PART IV

Dating/Romance Shows

"Will you accept this rose?"
—Rose ceremony mantra,
The Bachelor and *The Bachelorette*

On dating/romance shows, cameras follow aspiring lovebirds to record the mating play-by-play. Whether you're looking for true love or just a good laugh, you'll heart these reality TV shows for sure.

AVERAGE JOE

If you audition for *Average Joe*, chances are you won't even know it. You see, when you build a show around the idea of "average-looking guys" (which most people take to mean "ugly-looking guys"), you tend to have a hard time getting people to show up at your casting calls. Which is why the casting directors at *Average Joe* usually hide the truth about their show until the final round of the auditioning process.

During the show's first two seasons, none of the applicants knew the show was *Average Joe* until they were in the finals. For Season 3, in response to the show's popularity, the network allowed the casting directors—right before the finals—to tell all potential cast members that they were indeed auditioning for *Average Joe*.

STAT SHEET

PREMISE:
A stunning beauty queen arrives in paradise expecting a group of potential Prince Charmings to vie for her heart. When the men arrive, however, she learns that the handsome princes are actually "Average Joes"—nice guys with average looks. The midseason twist? After she's grown attached to the Average Joes, a bunch of hotties arrives to stir up the pot. Who will she end up falling for?

HOST:
Kathy Griffin

NETWORK:
NBC

YEARS RUNNING:
Season 1 premiered in November 2003.
As of December 2004, three seasons have aired.

CONTACT:
NBC—Web: *www.nbc.com*

EXECUTIVE PRODUCERS:
Stuart Krasnow, Andrew Glassman

CONTESTANT AGE RANGE:
21 and up

NUMBER OF APPLICANTS PER SEASON:
15,000

NUMBER OF CONTESTANTS:
Sixteen to twenty guys, one girl

The Audition Process

This type of show is a little tricky, because the casting team won't advertise right off the bat that it's auditioning candidates for *Average Joe*. When the show announces upcoming casting calls—which it does on NBC's Web site (*www.nbc.com*), on local NBC affiliates during prime time, or on morning radio shows—the pitch will probably sound something like this:

NBC is looking for guys to come out and audition for our latest reality TV show. The show will be similar to the movie *Animal House*, but will also have a wild and fun dating/competition element. It'll be set in an exotic location, with some fabulous prizes to be won! We're looking for all types of males, ages twenty-five to thirty-five, so come on down!

That's basically how the casting team promoted the first three seasons of the show. And I'm not making up the whole *Animal House* thing, either—it probably helps them get the frat-type guys who've now grown up and gotten a smidge homelier.

The reason they don't say "Hey uglies, avert your eyes from your computer for five minutes and hunchback your way over to our casting call!" is that the casting department isn't casting *only* "average" guys—they're also on the lookout for hunky, male-model types. So when they say they're looking for *all* types, they really mean *all* types.

Average Joe does not use videotaped applications in its casting process; to be cast, you must either attend an open call or be recruited off the street.

Open Casting Calls

Average Joe's open casting calls consist of one-on-one interviews with a casting director and a video camera. I'm told that the interviews are pretty brief—five minutes, in and out. The casting directors simply want to see what you look like—how "average" you are or how "hot" you are—and get a feel for your personality.

The interviews at these calls aren't very in-depth—candidates with successful interviews will be passed on to the next round within five minutes—because the nature of the show doesn't require it. After all, it's not like *The Real World*, where the cast members have to be on camera entertaining millions of people for six months straight. Because this is a dating show with a pool of twenty men who will be eliminated one by one, many of these guys are going to last only twenty minutes, or a few episodes at most—even if they're ultimately chosen to be on the show.

You can expect the majority of questions in your interview to focus on past dating experiences, what kind of girls you like, and what you do for fun. They keep it light.

Round Two and Beyond

Once the street recruiting and open casting calls are completed, the casting directors get together and, out of the one to two thousand applicants, pick their favorite thirty-five to forty guys as finalists. There are no second or third or fourth interviews here; if they like you after five minutes, and they think you'd make a good member of a cast, the casting directors will send you to L.A. for the finals.

The *Average Joe* finals follow the reality-TV casting formula pretty closely (aside from the fact that you'll still have no idea what show you're auditioning for). Expect a series of psychological evaluations and medical tests. And since it's a dating show, make sure you're STD-free—dating shows tend to be *very* serious about this requirement, and *Average Joe* is no exception. No matter how great a contestant you might be, if you have a sexually transmitted disease, you're done.

By the end of the week, you'll have sat through a few more interviews with casting directors and network executives, and soon they'll let you know whether you're off to exotic locations to win fabulous prizes.

Want to Be the Girl on Average Joe?

Well, it's not so easy. For the most part, the casting team selects actresses or models who haven't had too much exposure—unusually pretty girls whom you've never seen before. The casting directors tell me that the ideal candidate is "healthy, good-looking, smart—a universal beauty queen. She has to be the kind of girl that every guy would be attracted to."

Also, make sure you've never done any "nude work." The show had a girl lined up for Season 2 until, a few days before shooting, they found out she had done a topless scene in a popular teen comedy. Oops! The casting team had to find another girl.

So, if you think you've got what it takes to pick and choose amongst the Average Joes, the only advice I can give you is. . . have your agent call their people!

WHAT THEY'RE LOOKING FOR

The *Average Joe* casting directors tell me that there are three types of guys they're looking for:

1. Super-Duper Average: These guys epitomize the word "dork." We're talking glasses, weird hair, snorting when they laugh, leaking pens in pockets—you get the idea.

2. Real Average: You know these guys—they're like your friends. They work at software companies, they're pretty normal looking, they have good senses of humor, maybe a little love-handle action. You know . . . average.

3. Not Average At All: These are the hunks (did I actually say "hunk"?)—the male models, the typical good-looking TV guys, the extreme opposites of the guys in the previous two categories.

If you think you fit into one of these categories, then *Average Joe* is your show.

Of course, within these three categories of guys there are also subcategories, but I won't go into them too much. Let's just say that if you cast ten computer nerds on one show, and all they do is talk about computers, it doesn't make for very good television. So the casting team has to spice up the mix by finding a variety of guys within each of the three categories.

One of the nice things about *Average Joe* is that, unlike many other reality shows, the show doesn't cast *just* type A personalities. The casting directors don't shy away from wallflowers or more socially awkward types—in fact, they love them! So if you're not the loudest guy at your weekly Dungeons & Dragons match, don't worry about it! You've still got a chance!

Did You Know?

Hiding the truth about a reality show can be a daunting task for the casting directors, especially when they're casting "computer geeks." During the casting process for Season 2, one guy made it all the way to the finals, only to get disqualified for hacking into NBC's computer system and figuring out the show for which he was actually auditioning! Once the casting directors found out that he knew, they had to hustle him out the door lickity-split, before he spilled the beans to the other potential cast members.

What About Average Jane?

As the popularity of *Average Joe* increased, people started wondering when *Average Jane* might pop up on their television screens. In fact, thousands of E-mails were sent to NBC by girls who, having watched *Average Joe*, wished to plead their cases as potential "Average Janes" should the network ever decide to create such a show. Well, the network took the hint and cast the show. They found Average Janes from all over the country—mostly through word of mouth, since they were well aware that not too many women would show up to a casting call looking for "average" girls, and through street recruiting, which to me sounds even more difficult than holding a casting call. Imagine walking up to a woman on the street and telling her you think she's "average." Ouch! But apparently enough women thought the show would be a blast—after all, who wouldn't want to party at an exotic location on NBC's dime and show a bunch of "hot girls" who's boss? So in the summer of 2004, *Average Jane* began casting.

Unfortunately, NBC backed out on the deal—even after an entire *Average Jane* cast had been assembled—and for now the future of *Average Jane* hangs in limbo. Sigh.

Bachelor Byron Velvick
with the season 6 cast
(photo courtesy of ABC)

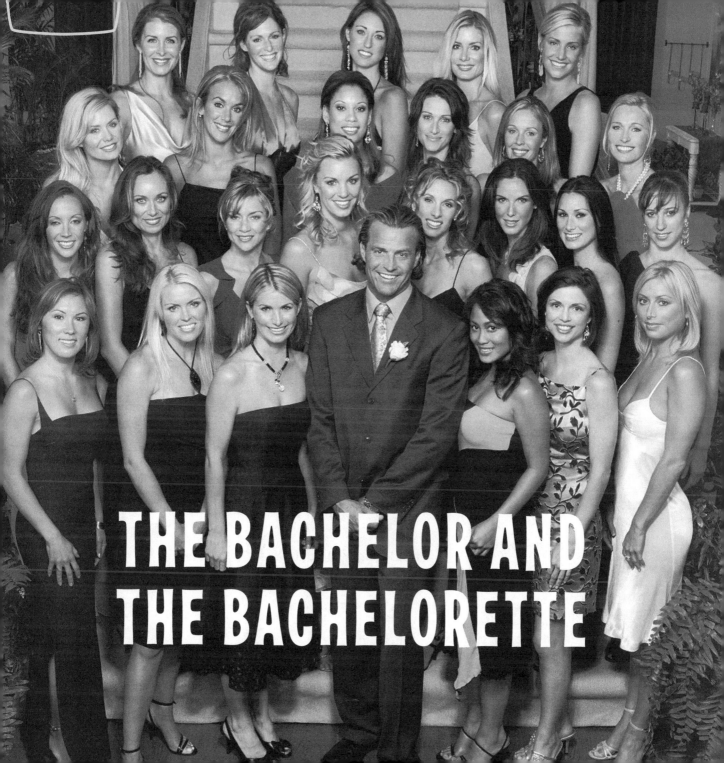

THE BACHELOR AND
THE BACHELORETTE

STAT SHEET

PREMISE:
Twenty-five single women vie for the
attention of one very eligible bachelor, or
vice versa, in the hopes of finding true love.

HOST:
Chris Harrison

NETWORK:
ABC

YEARS RUNNING:
Seven seasons of *The Bachelor*,
three seasons of *The Bachelorette*

CONTACT:
Web: *www.abc.com*
Phone: (866) 739–3151

PRODUCTION COMPANY:
Next Entertainment, Telepictures Productions

CREATOR:
Mike Fleiss

EXECUTIVE PRODUCER:
Mike Fleiss

CONTESTANT AGE RANGE:
21 and up

**NUMBER OF APPLICANTS
PER SEASON:**
25,000

NUMBER OF CONTESTANTS CHOSEN:
Usually twenty-five men/women and one
bachelor/bachelorette

Looking for love in all the wrong places? Think you could find true love in front of a national television audience? Then *The Bachelor* or *The Bachelorette* is the show for you. Since both *The Bachelor* and *The Bachelorette* are produced and cast by the same people, the processes are nearly identical, save for a few minor details that I'll explain later.

The Bachelor/Bachelorette takes a group of singles, throws them into a house, and periodically sends them on either individual or group dates with the Bachelor/Bachelorette. At the end of each week the Bachelor/Bachelorette hands out roses to those whom they feel a potential love connection with. Those left standing rose-less are sent to find love elsewhere while the remaining singles battle it out to see who will make it to the final two and be given a chance to ask for the Bachelor/Bachelorette's hand in marriage.

Whether you want to fight your way to true love as one of the twenty-five contestants on the show, or think you're better suited to have your pick of the litter as the Bachelor or Bachelorette, this chapter will put you in the best possible position by arming you with all the information necessary to find true love the twenty-first century way: on prime time!

The Audition Process

According to the casting directors with whom I spoke, the first few seasons of *The Bachelor* were very difficult to cast. Most people found the idea of finding true

Chris Harrison, host of *The Bachelor* and *The Bachelorette* (photo courtesy of ABC)

love on a reality show laughable. It wasn't until it was time to cast the third season that tapes started pouring into the production offices, and thousands of people began turning up at open casting calls.

The immense popularity of the *Bachelor/Bachelorette* series has made them the Rolls-Royce of season-long dating shows—and, as a result, one of the hardest reality shows on which to land a spot. But have no fear my lovelorn friends: Cupid's arrow favors the well-prepared. Read on with stalwart heart!

To find out if the show is casting, either check the ABC Web site (*www.abc.com*) or watch ABC during prime time for up-to-the-minute casting information from your local ABC affiliate.

The Bachelor/Bachelorette's popularity has made street recruiting a thing of the past for the casting department, leaving video applications and open calls as the only ways to get cast.

Video Application

Can't get down to an open call? Well, have no fear: More than half of the people who ended up on past seasons of *The Bachelor/Bachelorette* have gotten there by submitting video applications.

Your video should be between two and five minutes long. Sit in plain view of the camera, speak clearly, and state in a conversational fashion your name, occupation, where you live, and why should you be chosen to appear on *The Bachelor/Bachelorette*.

As a side note, *The Bachelor* and *Bachelorette* are two of the few shows that rely heavily on friend recommendations during their casting processes. Do you have a friend who you think would be perfect for *The Bachelor/Bachelorette*, but who would never in a million years apply on their own? Well, do it for them!

If you're going to recommend a friend, the casting people want to see both you and your friend on camera together. The best way to do this is to interview the friend you're nominating, asking him or her the same questions you would answer in your own video application, such as why this person would make a perfect contestant on the show, what positive attributes you think they possess, and what this person is looking for in a mate. So if you think your friend would be great on *The Bachelor/Bachelorette*, then get over to his or her house right now, camera in hand, and surprise-attack him or her with an impromptu interview! The casting directors love that kind of stuff.

Open Casting Call

For up-to-date information about the dates and locations of open casting calls, check the ABC Web site or keep your eyes open while watching your local ABC affiliate.

Once you're standing in line at the open call, you'll be asked to fill out a short application, which will ask you for general background information such as your name, age, occupation, marital status, and whether you have children. Once you're inside, the open call will consist of a one-on-one filmed interview with a casting associate.

SEND YOUR PACKAGE TO:

★ ★

If the shows are casting, visit the ABC Web site (www.abc.com) *to download the short application you must submit with your video. When your package is ready, mail it to:*

★ ★

The Bachelor/Bachelorette Casting
14622 Ventura Blvd #1019
Sherman Oaks, CA 91403

★ ★

Bachelorette Jen Schefft with the cast from Season 3 (photo courtesy of ABC)

Expect to answer the following questions: Why do you want to be on *The Bachelor/Bachelorette*? What were some of your past relationships like? What kind of person are you looking for? Would you be willing to get married if you were the final person chosen on the show? Do you believe in love at first sight? Do you think you could fall in love with someone and marry them after knowing them for only five weeks?

Sound like a lot of questions? Well, try answering them in under five minutes, which is how long each person gets at a *Bachelor/Bachelorette* open call. Given the short time frame, you're going to have to be very economical with your answers. Have a friend ask you the questions a few times for practice before you go into the casting call. Make sure your answers are short and to the point, while still giving your personality a chance to shine.

Round Two And Beyond

After viewing thousands of tapes and conducting thousands of open-call interviews, the casting team selects one hundred people to fill out the "long application," which lives up to its name at thirty-five pages. It asks you about everything—from your blood type to your exes' phone numbers and addresses. Yes, you heard me: Your past flames will be contacted by the casting department and asked questions about their relationships with you. Basically, the casting department needs to find out if you've ever had any restraining orders filed against you, or if you've had an abusive past. After they've weeded out the psychos, the casting team will select a final group of fifty to be flown out to Los Angeles.

The finals process on *The Bachelor/Bachelorette* is a very quick one, lasting only one to two days. During that time, the sequestered final fifty will meet with the show's producers, be interviewed at length, undergo medical and psychological testing, and submit to extensive background checks by a private investigator to

WHAT THEY'RE LOOKING FOR

Although the criteria for contestants change slightly every year, *The Bachelor* and *Bachelorette* generally look for twenty-one- to thirty-year-old single people who have never been divorced and have no children.

The "no children" rule has remained hard-and-fast since the show's first season. According to the casting directors, the producers made the rule when the show began, based on two assumptions: first, that it would be painful for a child to watch his or her parent get rejected; and second, that the show should not be responsible for separating a parent from his or her child for six weeks. Bottom line: If you've got children, *The Bachelor/Bachelorette* is not the show for you.

The "no divorce" rule, however, seems to be less strictly enforced. The producers used to prohibit divorcees from appearing on the show, but when they met Bob from Season Four, they quickly changed the rule because he was such an impressive candidate for *The Bachelor*. Byron from Season Six was also a divorcee— so unless the casting department changes its policy for future seasons, it seems that having been divorced is no longer a deal breaker.

For the final group of twenty-five contestants—both women on *The Bachelor* and men on *The Bachelorette*—the casting department is looking for a diverse group of people. They want varying levels of financial success, varying body types, and varying personalities. The only criterion they're looking for across the board is an entertaining personality; a contestant must have the ability to captivate a viewing audience. Remember, the producers aren't just trying to make a love connection here—above all, they're trying to make a television show. An entertaining personality is essential to achieving that goal.

Aside from that, the casting directors look for people who really want to fall in love. They want the show to mean something to each and every person they cast, so the first thing they ask themselves when interviewing a potential cast member or watching a videotaped application is, "Does this person just want to be on TV, or does he or she really want to fall in love?"

If you believe in finding love and think you could do it on network television, then get out there with your heart on your sleeve, be as real and honest as you can be, and let your personality wow them. Good luck!

WHAT THEY'RE LOOKING FOR IN A BACHELOR OR BACHELORETTE

For those who want to be *the* Bachelor or Bachelorette, things get a little more specific. Although the process used to cast the Bachelor/Bachelorette is the same as the process used to cast the other twenty-five contestants, the way in which the casting department has selected the Bachelor/Bachelorette has been different almost every season. The most consistent bet is to have a friend nominate you to be on the show. Moreover, the casting directors tell me that they like their Bachelors and Bachelorettes to need some convincing before they commit to the kingly/queenly role—I guess it makes them seem a bit more humble.

For the Bachelor, the casting directors prefer a slightly different type of person from the type of person who will become the Bachelorette (aside from the obvious differences). The Bachelor must be a successful, All-American, self-made man. He doesn't necessarily need to have a six-figure income, but he also can't work at McDonald's (no offense to the army of McDonald's employees nationwide, but boxing up Chicken McNuggets an eligible bachelor does not make). Success, attractiveness, and an outgoing personality are key.

When it first cast the Bachelorette, the casting department was hoping to find an equally successful woman—a sexy CEO type—but was unable to find the right woman within the required time frame. Thus the role of Bachelorette was opened up to women everywhere, and a great personality and pretty face became her most important attributes for casting purposes.

determine whether they have any outstanding warrants, if they've ever been convicted of any crimes, or if they've ever spent any time in jail.

Of the people who pass these tests with flying colors, twenty-five will be selected as contestants and one will be chosen as the Bachelor/Bachelorette.

Did You Know?

As of now the only two Bachelor couples not to break up after their seasons finished taping are Byron and Mary from Bachelor 6 and Charlie and Sarah from Bachelor 7.

On the flipside, only Trista from Bachelorette 1 has been able to maintain her relationship with her beau, Ryan. That makes the Bachelor/Bachelorette success rate two-out-of-seven for the guys and one-out-of-three for the girls. Not exactly the best odds I've ever heard.

Good luck Charlie, Byron and Trista!

BLIND DATE

STAT SHEET

PREMISE:
Two people go out on a blind date in the hopes of making a love connection, while *Pop-Up Video*–style wisecracks appear on-screen to make light of their—more often than not, uncomfortably bad—date.

HOST:
Roger Lodge

NETWORK:
Syndication, check local listings

YEARS RUNNING:
First aired in 1999

CONTACT:
Web: *www.blinddatetv.com*

PRODUCTION COMPANY:
Universal Television

EXECUTIVE PRODUCERS:
David Garfinkle, Thomas Klein, Matthew Papish, Jay Renfroe

CONTESTANT AGE RANGE:
21 and up

NUMBER OF APPLICANTS PER SEASON:
5,000

NUMBER OF CONTESTANTS CHOSEN:
Two per date, around thirty per season

One of the shows that started the reality-TV phenomenon, and surely the first true reality-TV dating show, *Blind Date* is, and always will be, the king of reality-TV love. Whereas past dating shows asked couples to describe their dates to an audience after the fact, *Blind Date* brings the audience along for the ride—letting them see for themselves the good, the bad, and the ugly of modern romance.

Whether it's someone storming off in the middle of dinner or awkwardly begging for a kiss at the end of the night, the antics featured on *Blind Date* have held viewers' attention longer than any other reality TV show on the air. And since the show has been picked up for syndication in more television markets than I even knew existed, it will most likely continue to captivate audiences for many, many years to come. Want to be a part of America's number-one dating show? Here's how.

The Audition Process

Casting-wise, *Blind Date* is one of the more accessible reality TV shows on the air. As long as you're single, over twenty-one, and outgoing, you stand a fine chance of getting cast on the show. There's no age cut-off either, so all you grandmas and grandpas out there need not feel left out. The audition process varies slightly depending on whether you live in Los Angeles or elsewhere, but it's simple either way. Listen close now.

If you live in the Los Angeles area, auditioning for *Blind Date* is about as easy as can be. Simply go to the show's Web site (*www.blinddatetv.com*) and click on the little star icon that reads "Star on *Blind Date*." This will take you to a short application consisting of a handful of basic questions—name, age, sex, occupation—and a few short-answer essay questions. Some of the highlights include: "What celebrities do you resemble?" and "What is the wildest thing you've ever done?"

Every person who completes an online application receives a phone call from a *Blind Date* casting associate, who will conduct a quick interview with you over the phone. As long as you're single, over twenty-one, and have an outgoing personality, the casting person will then invite you to the show's offices for an interview.

If you don't live in L.A., you'll still have a chance to attend open casting calls, because *Blind Date* likes to travel. A lot. The show films episodes all over the world, sending wild couples on hilarious dates all the way from Ibiza, Spain, to New Orleans, Louisiana.

The best way to know if and when the show will be coming to your neck of the woods is to watch the show itself. If they're planning on shooting a few dates in your town in the near future, the casting department will post an announcement at the end of an episode telling you where to go and what to do.

Blind Date open calls consist of a bunch of people coming to a public venue such as a bar or a restaurant, mingling with other applicants, filling out quick applications, and having quick interviews with someone from the *Blind Date* casting department. If the casting team likes your interview and application, they'll take down your information and contact you fairly soon after the open call.

Boys and girls are interviewed on different days, so they don't get a chance to see one another (hence the word "blind" in the show's title), but most likely you'll be able to audition within a few days of submitting your application online.

At the audition, you'll complete a seven-page application asking you a few more-detailed questions about your life, including questions relating to past dating experiences and the qualities you're looking for in a mate. You'll then be brought in for a filmed interview, which can last anywhere from five to forty-five minutes.

During the filmed interview, the casting director will ask questions based on the answers you provided in your seven-page application. So if you wrote in your application that your worst date ever was with a woman who turned out to be a space monster, the casting director would most likely start the interview by saying "So, it says here that you went on a date with a space monster. What was that like?"

The interview is very conversational and relaxed—and, from what I hear, kinda fun. *Blind Date* has a good staff that's been casting for a *very* long time, so they really know how to make the audition process a good experience for all involved.

Your best bet for the interview is just to be yourself—as long as being yourself means being outgoing, interesting, and dynamic.

Round Two and Beyond

All it takes is one interview. If the casting team likes you, they'll contact you anywhere from one day to three months after your interview—and if you get a call from them, it means you're on the show. When they call, they'll let you know the date and location of your big date, and that's it. You're on TV. So easy!

Did You Know?

Blind Date as we know it today actually took its name from one of reality TV's very first dating shows, also called *Blind Date*, which aired in 1949 and was hosted by Melvyn Douglas. The original *Blind Date* took in-studio audience members who had written into the show describing their dream date, coupled them up with their perfect in-studio matches, and sent them both out on a night they'd never forget. Something tells me the 1949 version of *Blind Date* never ended in a Jacuzzi with a topless girl and some guy yelling "cocktail!"

WHAT THEY'RE LOOKING FOR

The requirements couldn't be more straightforward: You've got to be single, over the age of twenty-one, and outgoing. That's pretty much it. And the show isn't even that picky when it comes to looks—the casting team likes to cast people of all shapes and types. Better still, the show also isn't picky about age. In fact, the oldest person ever to appear on *Blind Date* was a whopping ninety-two years old. Seriously! A ninety-two-year-old man was sent on a date with an eighty-one-years-young lady. He did push ups and sang for her, and it was very cute. The night even ended with a kiss and a promise of more dates! So if you've got even the slightest inkling that you'd like to apply for *Blind Date*, there is really no reason to hesitate—you've got a good chance of making it onto the show.

Interview
Harley Tat, Former Executive Producer of *Blind Date*

MR: How did you become involved with *Blind Date*?

> HT: I was brought on as a show runner when the show was in a presentation stage. The show got sold to PolyGram, which eventually became Universal Worldwide Television. I came on as the head writer and show runner, serving as the supervising producer in the beginning, and for the last three years I was the executive producer. I was with the show for one thousand episodes and five years.

MR: When the show first started out, how did you find people for the show and what were you looking for?

> HT: We put together a casting department who canvassed all of Los Angeles, Orange County, Burbank, nightclubs, 10K races, restaurants, festivals, everywhere. A team of recruiters went out and got the numbers and bodies to come in here, put them on tape, and had them fill out an extended questionnaire. Then we make the determination as to a) were they suitable for the show; and b) if they were, which person would we pair them up with?

MR: Has the process changed much over the years?

> HT: It's pretty much the same. But you see, *Blind Date* was the first of this new wave of reality shows. I think it was really groundbreaking. It put real people out there in real situations, in a kind of fishbowl environment, and took a look at their behavior.
>
> I think that the casting in the beginning was much more innocent and pure then it is now. Once a show gets on the air, people are a lot more cognizant of just that: being on television. In the beginning of the show, the reason the show was successful was you saw real people in real situations, unfazed by the cameras. We'd go out with these people for twelve to fifteen hours, and after the first ten minutes they'd forget the cameras were there. They would be themselves. Guys that were

assholes were assholes, and girls that were—excuse the phrase—bitches, were bitches. Their true colors came out on tape.

Now with the whole advent of these Reality stars getting spreads in *Playboy* and *Maxim* and being on TV shows, I think it's drawn more of the actor and actress type that wants to be in front of the camera.

MR: *Blind Date* was one of the first reality shows to have a sense of humor about itself. How do you think *Blind Date* has affected reality TV as a whole?

HT: I've always said *Blind Date* is a relationship comedy show, and comedy always cuts through. If you can provide a show that is entertaining and funny, then people will consistently watch it. When people watch *Blind Date*, they become addicted to the comedic bubbles over people's heads, and to the lower thirds and the different characters that we put on-screen. They wanted to see what the characters were going to say and the thoughts we were going to put in people's heads. I think that comedy is a very important element to reality TV. We were the first to do that and do it successfully.

MR: What advice would you give to someone who wanted to be on *Blind Date*? What makes a great contestant?

HT: They need to be themselves and come with no expectations. I was in forms of reality TV before *Blind Date*. I used to produce *Hard Copy*, *Extra*, and *A Current Affair*. Those news magazine shows used to be called reality television, before what we now consider reality TV even existed.

But working in this new wave of reality TV, I was really shocked at just how mean men and women can be to each other on television. I think that it's a display of the fact that they actually forget the cameras are there. Men and women on *Blind Date* become really mean to each other in very short amounts of time. You'll see it even when they first open the door; right away, if they don't like the way that person looks, they go out to the car and the woman immediately starts trashing the guy, or vice versa. That behavior was surprising to me. Rather than just go through the date, be pleasant, and at the end say "No, thank you," right away these guys start going at it. I was really blown away by that.

To answer your question, if you want to be on the show, you should have a unique personality, a unique look, and be yourself. If you're acting or you're posing, it won't cut it on television and we won't put you on the air.

MR: In all your years on *Blind Date*, do you have a personal favorite date or moment?

HT: There's been a lot of major characters on the show that have been very memorable. I really liked our first couple of seasons, when the show was becoming part of the American consciousness. Jay Leno was talking about it, it was getting a lot of buzz, and you could kind of see it starting to stick. People were coming out of the woodwork to try and be on the show. It was not only innocent and genuine for the people who came on the show—it was innocent and genuine for us as producers, because it was a really special show that combined a kind of comic-strip mentality with the relationship genre. It had never been done before, and to see that take hold and be successful was really exciting.

We took the show to various spots around the country. To come into Austin or Phoenix and see the buzz around the show was really cool. That was an exciting time. We took the show international to Ibiza, Spain. It was interesting to put it in another country and see what happened. I also executive-produced a show called *The Fifth Wheel* for three seasons, which was like the sister show of *Blind Date*. I did five hundred episodes of that show.

MR: Where do you think reality TV is going next?

HT: Reality TV is changing very fast. Packaging is where it's at. A normal idea isn't really worth much anymore, unless it's attached to either a celebrity or a high-profile executive. I think that reality TV has replaced the kind of shows you had in the seventies—shows by Spelling and Bochco and all these big drama companies. There's about six to ten mini-studios of reality TV right now, and they're taking over that drama niche that was popular in the seventies and eighties.

Everything is packaging: it's putting the right talent, the right backing, and a big budget together. Nowadays, reality-TV-show budgets can be between $1 and $2 million for an hour. We did *Blind Date* for between $150,000 and $225,000 for a week's worth of shows. People are willing to pay a lot for an hour of prime-time reality TV now.

The one thing that hasn't been successful is anything that is too mean-spirited, or that victimizes someone—the audience tunes out to that stuff. I also think the whole elimination thing is going out. It's becoming more documentary style. All the shows look the same now—everyone lives in a house and gets eliminated each week, and I think that's on its way out.

MR: What do you think originally drew people to be on *Blind Date*, and do you think it's changed at all now?

HT: I think relationships and dating are timeless. Even if they don't think they're looking for love, everyone is. Whether it's in a relationship with a man or a woman, or having pets, or a family, or a job, everyone is looking to be loved.

When you can tell a guy "Hey, come on our show—we're going to hook you up with a hot girl and you're going to be on TV," there's nothing better. You know, Internet dating used to be a taboo. When you heard that someone met someone on the Internet, you'd say "God, what a couple of losers!" But now it's very mainstream. It just goes to show you that people are really looking to hook up, and the goal of *Blind Date* has always been to hook people up. Some people think we just hook people up to fail, but we actually hook people up to connect. They fail on their own.

Harley Tat is one of reality TV's leading producers, having produced for A Current Affair, Hard Copy, Extra, Blind Date, *and* The Fifth Wheel. *Harley has a slew of new, top-secret reality shows coming soon to a television near you.*

STAT SHEET

PREMISE:
It's survival of the fittest in the dating world, as four suitors vie for the attention of one lucky single.

HOST:
Kerry McFadden

NETWORK:
WB

YEARS RUNNING:
First aired in September 2001

CONTACT:
Web: *elimidate.warnerbros.com/*

PRODUCTION COMPANY:
Dawn Syndicated Productions, in association with Telepictures Productions

CREATOR:
Alex Duda

EXECUTIVE PRODUCER:
Alex Duda

CONTESTANT AGE RANGE:
21 and up

NUMBER OF APPLICANTS PER SEASON:
2,000

NUMBER OF CONTESTANTS CHOSEN:
one single, four suitors per episode, twenty-five episodes in a season

ELIMIDATE

If the average televised dating show lacks the rivalry and verbal abuse you demand from your filmed dating experiences, then *Elimidate* might just be the show for you.

Like an entire season of *The Bachelor/Bachelorette* on fast-forward, *Elimidate* takes a group of men or women and has them vie for the attention of one suitor. At each stage of the date one member of the harem is eliminated until finally the group is pared down to one (hopefully) happy couple. Throw in a bit of verbal squabbling and the occasional body-shot and you've got *Elimidate*.

The Audition Process

The *Elimidate* casting process is pretty run-of-the-mill. First, visit *elimidate.warnerbros.com* and click on "Do You Want to Be on the Show?" From there you'll be instructed either to send the casting department an E-mail, or to check for open calls in your area. If the show's going to be casting in your town, this information will be posted on the Web site. If not, you might as well send an E-mail so the casting team will have you on file when they *do* come to your area. If you live in the Los Angeles area, your best bet is to send an E-mail to arrange an interview with the casting department.

SEND YOUR PACKAGE TO:

★ ★ ★ ★ ★ ★ ★ ★ ★ ★ ★ ★ ★ ★ ★ ★ ★ ★ ★ ★

Elimidate Casting
P.O. Box 1645
Burbank, CA 91507-1645

★ ★ ★ ★ ★ ★ ★ ★ ★ ★ ★ ★ ★ ★ ★ ★ ★ ★ ★ ★

After you've submitted your application, as long as you don't look like Eric Stoltz's character from the movie Mask, *you'll most likely receive a phone call from someone in the* Elimidate *casting department. If you live in the L.A. area, he or she will then ask you to come in for an interview.*

By E-mail

To apply electronically, send an E-mail to elimidate@wb.com with your name, age, occupation, address, and two phone numbers. You should also attach a recent photo of yourself in JPEG format, no larger than 800 x 600 pixels. And if what I just said sounds like meaningless jargon to you, ask your friendly, neighborhood computer geek to help you out with it.

Your best bet is to send *two* photos: one close-up and one full-body shot. And the fewer clothes you have on in the full-body shot, the better, but don't go nude—it's not *that* kind of show. Well, it kind of is, but you know what I mean.

I can't for the life of me imagine why you'd want to do this, but you can also send the above information to the casting department by regular mail. If you're the last person on earth to use E-mail, then this might be the way to go for you.

Open Call

Elimidate open calls are usually pretty casual. They often take place at bars, and involve filling out a short form, having a quick conversation with an *Elimidate* casting person, getting a Polaroid photo taken, and possibly getting hammered and leaving with a stranger. But that's just what I've heard.

Round Two and Beyond

If the casting directors like your application, they'll call you in for an interview. The interview will consist of you and a casting director acting like a couple of Chatty Kathys—talking all about your past dating experiences and what you're looking for in a mate. Just be yourself, be personable, and have fun.

Somewhere between one day and three months after your interview, a casting person may call to say that you've made it onto the show. In which case, put on your sexiest outfit, sharpen up those claws, and come out swinging. Game on!

What They're Looking For

Elimidate is looking for aggressive, fun, wild people who aren't afraid to be themselves on-camera. And since it's a competition as well as a dating show, you've got to be able to prove to the casting team that you're not going to crawl into the fetal position and cry the minute someone tries to cut you down. In fact, insulting the other contestants is a big part of what makes the show entertaining to viewers—so make sure you're as good at dishing it out as you are at taking it.

The bottom line: *Elimidate* looks for contestants with big, fun, over-the-top personalities and good dating experience. And if you're a lady, showing a little skin never hurts. Wait. . . did I just say that out loud?

Did You Know?

Elimidate claims to be responsible for the very first reality TV couple ever to have gotten married after meeting on their show. That's right, Mequasah and Billy met on an episode of *Elimidate* and later ended up at the altar together.

PART V

Talent-Based Shows

"If you had lived two thousand years ago
and sung like that, I think they would have stoned you."
—Simon Cowell, *American Idol*

Talent-based shows are not your average reality TV shows:
They demand more from their contestants. On these shows, artists and wannabe
superstars have a real shot at money and fame.

STAT SHEET

PREMISE:
Fourteen beautiful young girls compete in a series of "model activities," battling it out for a contract at a top modeling agency.

HOST:
Tyra Banks

NETWORK:
UPN

YEARS RUNNING:
Season 1 debuted in May of 2003.

CONTACT:
UPN—Phone: (323) 575-7000
Web: *www.upn.com*

PRODUCTION COMPANY:
10 by 10 Entertaining, in association with Bankable Productions

CREATOR:
Tyra Banks

EXECUTIVE PRODUCERS:
Tyra Banks, Ken Mok

CONTESTANT AGE RANGE:
18–27

NUMBER OF APPLICANTS PER SEASON:
30,000

NUMBER OF CONTESTANTS CHOSEN:
Fourteen

AMERICA'S NEXT TOP MODEL

Welcome to every-girl-I-know's favorite reality TV show. Whether they love the chic fashions, the glamorous photo shoots, or the catty fights, the fans of *America's Next Top Model* can't get enough of this show.

ANTM takes a group of model-esque young girls with no formal modeling experience, throws them into a fancy house, and has them compete each week in photo shoots and other various model-friendly tasks. The photos, as well as the models themselves, are discussed by a panel of judges as one girl is eliminated from the running each week until one lucky girl is crowned "America's Next Top Model."

So what does it take to make it onto *America's Next Top Model*? Let's find out!

Photo courtesy of Adrianne Curry and Christopher Knight

The Audition Process

ANTM holds open calls and accepts video applications. Check the show's Web site to find out if and when it's casting, or look for a schedule of open-call auditions on your local UPN affiliate during prime time. If there are no open calls in your area, you'll need to apply with a video application.

Some things to know before we get started:

★ You must be between the ages of eighteen and twenty-seven.

★ You must be *at least* five feet, seven inches tall.

★ If accepted on the show, you may be *required* to pose clothed, partially clothed, or naked. Be prepared for this.

★ You must have had no experience as a model in a national campaign within the last five years. This includes appearances on TV and in print advertisements.

★ If you are cast on the show and you have an agent, you must immediately terminate your agent (I'm pretty sure they mean "fire," not "kill").

I know the majority of women out there are shorter than five-foot-seven, but from what I gather this is a non-negotiable requirement. But that's still not going to stop me from telling you to audition. If there's one thing I know about reality TV, it's that it loves to break its own rules. Who knows? You could be that perfect girl they're looking for—the one who'll teach them that vertically-challenged girls are just as model-friendly as the tall ones. Get 'em, girls!

Video Application

If you choose to audition using a video application, your tape must be three minutes long and in VHS format.

The question the casting department wants you to answer on your video application is: "Who are you, and why would you make the ultimate top model?"

Most reality TV shows recommend a shoulders-up, "talking-head" approach to filming your video application. But since your face and body are so important on *ANTM*, I definitely recommend that your entire physique be visible (clothed, of course) at some point during your three minute self-interview. Maybe start off with a catwalk toward the camera, then plop down and talk directly to the lens. Or halfway through your interview you might jump up and let them see what your momma gave you. However you decide to do it (creativity is key!), make sure that at some point the casting team gets a good look at you from top to bottom. (I'm talking about your feet here, people!)

Music is a big no-no in your video application. There is no quicker way to get a casting director to throw your tape into the trash than to spend half your tape dancing around to your favorite song. Even if you do a little catwalk in your video, do it in silence, or talk while doing it, but don't play any music. One reason casting directors hate music in application videos

SEND YOUR PACKAGE TO:

★★★★★★★★★★★★★★★★★★★★★

Gather your VHS video application, your completed fourteen-page application, your three photos, and a photocopy of your driver's license (or Social Security card with birth certificate), and address your package to:

★★★★★★★★★★★★★★★★★★★★★

America's Next Top Model [Region Code #]
2801 Ocean Park Blvd
Santa Monica, CA 90405

★★★★★★★★★★★★★★★★★★★★★

01. Northeast region
02. Southeast region
03. Northwest region
04. Southwest region
05. Midwest/Central region

is that, if you use music, they won't be able to use footage from your video on the show—for example, in a before/after clip—because they'll have to legally clear whatever music you used. Trust me: no music.

Most important, make sure you let your personality shine in your video. By the end of three minutes, you should have conveyed who you are and what you would add to the show. You should be entertaining, bigger than life, and confident. Let the very best version of yourself rise to the surface. You want to stand out, but you also don't want to showboat. And there's a thin line between putting your best foot forward and hamming it up for the camera, so make sure you don't come off as too pushy. Your videotape should communicate: This is who I am, this is how I became that person, and this is why you need me on your show. As they say in the biz, you've got to "pop" on-camera!

After you've made your video, download the fourteen-page application from the show's Web site and fill it out. Aside from the general age/occupation/location questions, expect to answer short-essay questions about your lifelong aspirations, modeling experience (if any), criminal record (if any), eating and drinking habits, and favorite supermodels.

In addition to your application, you'll need *three* photos of yourself. And not just any three photos—you must include

★ One close-up photo of your face.

★ One full-length photo of your entire (clothed) body.

★ One full-length photo of you in a swimsuit.

Don't ask me why, but one of these three photos *must* be in black and white. (The casting department leaves it up to you to decide which one.) The photos don't have to be of professional quality—Polaroids are acceptable, though I wouldn't use them if I were you. Try to use as nice a camera as possible to take your pictures; use your parents' old 35 mm camera, and have a friend light you nicely and snap a few great shots. Make a day of it and have some fun!

Your video application package is now ready to send! Drop it in the mail and start walking around your house with a book on your head. Why? Because it looks funny! And because you've got a lot of time to kill—it could take the show a few months to get back to you.

Open Calls

Before you head to an open call, make sure you bring the following items with you: a completed fourteen-page application (which can be downloaded from the *ANTM* Web site), three photos of yourself (see the "Video Application" section of this chapter for full details), and a photocopy of either your driver's license or Social Security card and birth certificate. If you don't have the fourteen-page application with you, the casting associates will give you one to fill out, but it's much smarter to have it filled out before you go.

Here's what to expect at the open call:

One by one, girls will be led in front of a camera and asked to give their names/ages/hometowns/occupations and then to answer the question: "Why would you make the ultimate top model?" Just as in the video application, you'll have only three minutes to tell them all about yourself.

Have your three minutes planned out before you arrive. You don't need to memorize a speech, which can come off looking overly rehearsed and unnatural, but you should at least have an idea of what you're going to say: what stories you're going to tell and what reasons you'll give as to why you should be on the show and why you want to be a model.

There is no perfect three-minute audition. Every girl who has made it on *ANTM* has done it a different way, which is part of the point: The casting department wants to see something new and refreshing. They want to be bowled over by you. You've got to stand in front of their camera and wow them. Try telling them a story they'll never forget, something hilarious or shocking. You want to have that casting associate sitting down at lunch with the rest of the casting department saying "you guys will never believe this story one girl told me." Being memorable is extremely important.

I'm told that, at some open calls, girls are also asked to do a little catwalking. This doesn't take place at every open call, but be prepared for it when you arrive. Practice a bit at home, and make sure you don't wear any shoes you're going to fall over in. Talk about embarrassing!

After the casting associates get your three minutes on tape, you're free to leave. And don't be discouraged if they don't come chasing after you in the parking lot—sometimes it takes a few months for them to decide who makes it to the semifinals.

Round Two and Beyond

If the casting department likes your open-call audition or video application, you'll be asked to come back to an as-yet-undetermined city in your region for a long interview. This interview will last about thirty minutes. Be warned: The show will not cover your expenses for the semifinals, so transportation and accommodations come out of your own pocket for this stretch of the audition process.

Your thirty-minute interview will be based on a long application you'll be required to fill out before you arrive. The long application will be filled with essay questions about nearly every aspect of your life and, in your thirty-minute interview, the casting team will ask you either to repeat or to expand upon the answers you give.

The casting people are trying to learn as much about you as possible, while at the same time seeing how well you react to being on-camera for an extended period of time.

Your long interview is not the time to clam up or act shy. Whoever you were in your video application or open-call audition, be that same person again. If it ain't broke, don't fix it.

If the casting people like your interview, they'll fly you to Los Angeles for a week of finals. Be prepared for extensive interviewing with the casting department, producers (yes, that means Tyra), and a few network executives. Medical examinations and psychological evaluations will also be given. If you make it past this round, you'll be on the show—and that much closer to being crowned America's Next Top Model. Congrats!

Did You Know?

Toccara from Season 3, the first plus-size model ever cast on *ANTM*, did not receive a callback after the first local casting call she attended—but that didn't stop her from going back for Round Two! She found out that the show was holding callbacks near her hometown and went on down there anyway. She said to herself, "You know what? I need to go there; as long as someone that has something to do with that show sees me, I'm going to be on that show." The casting directors were impressed by her determination, and the rest is reality-TV history.

WHAT THEY'RE LOOKING FOR

Let's get the basics out of the way. You've got to be drop-dead gorgeous. As important as personality is, let's not kid ourselves here—the show's looking for that small percentage of girls with the "model look." There are lots of beautiful girls in the world but, as Tyra has said many times, "we're not looking for cheerleaders"; they're looking for supermodels.

Most supermodels set themselves apart with some sort of bizarre physical trait: Tyra has a giant forehead, Cindy Crawford has her mole, Kate Moss has her invisibility when she turns sideways. Now, I have no idea why some girls are considered supermodels and some are just considered beautiful, but apparently the casting department at *America's Next Top Model* thinks they do. Don't take whatever they say personally, though. Remember: It's just a game show, and is not a real reflection on how beautiful you are.

As important as looks are on the show, however, the casting department still has thirteen hours of television to make entertaining, so personality is definitely a big factor in their casting process. So be yourself, be entertaining, and let them know what kind of person you are. Whether you're feisty and confrontational or innocent and reserved, show the casting team what "type" of model you're going to be on their show. Make it obvious and keep it entertaining. Most important, have fun with it. Nothing is more contagious in the world of reality-TV casting than an auditioner who's having a blast while auditioning. Good luck, ladies!

Interview
Adrianne Curry, *America's Next Top Model 1* and *The Surreal Life 4* and Christopher Knight, *The Brady Bunch* and *The Surreal Life 4*

Let me preface this interview a bit by saying my original intention was to interview Adrianne Curry about her experience auditioning for *America's Next Top Model*. With the success of her role on *The Surreal Life 4* I was even more excited to interview her and get her take on the extended world of reality TV. During the filming of *The Surreal Life 4* Adrianne fell in love with Christopher Knight (aka Peter Brady of *The Brady Bunch*). Icing on the cake: The following interview reveals both Adrianne's and Chris's perspective on the wild world of reality TV.

MR: How did you find out about *America's Next Top Model*?

Adrianne Curry: I was waitressing at a bar in Chicago and this guy who claimed to be a producer for UPN started telling me about the show. I figured he was just your typical scumbag trying to get me to come home with him so I threw all his information in the garbage. Shortly thereafter I saw a commercial for the show on TV and decided I should apply. I was worried because I was real close to the deadline, but I sent in my video even though I knew they were going to receive it late. I don't know why they watched it, but they did.

MR: What did you do on your video?

AC: It was about five to ten minutes (laughs). It was mayhem. I gave them a tour of my house. I showed them my family, which is really dysfunctional.

MR: Did you actually show the dysfunctional side of your family on the tape?

AC: Oh yeah. They saw it all. I didn't really care because I didn't think I'd get chosen. I did it just to entertain them, for the hell of it. Basically I gave them the rundown of myself. I showed them my bedroom, which is plastered with posters of the greatest bands of all time: The Doors, Led Zeppelin, Pink Floyd, The Who. I didn't dress up nice or anything, I just wore a spiked collar and a bandanna. I usually dress like a total butch, but obviously they saw something. To get on the show, I sometimes think it's not as much about looks as it is personality. They just want people to clash.

MR: How would you describe your attitude on the tape? Were you excited or subdued?

AC: It was just my typical midwestern deadpan delivery. Not really excited. I told the producers to "fuck-off" because it was cold in Chicago and warm in L.A. so I said "all you rich bastards sitting in the sun in L.A. can fuck off!"

MR: What happened after you sent the tape in?

AC: I figured it didn't get in because I missed the deadline, but I got a phone call a few weeks later saying I made the semifinals. After seeing so many thousands of women they picked twenty that they were going to fly out to L.A. I figured again: whatever.

I didn't bring nice clothes or anything. I went there and I looked like crap. I did the semifinals, which they air regardless of whether you make it onto the show or not; it's always the first episode. Then they picked me for the top ten based solely on personality, because they all thought I was ugly. Tyra (Banks) even said on the last show that she put a big "NO" next to my name because she didn't think I was pretty.

MR: What were the finals like in L.A.?

AC: A lot of nervousness. A lot of competition. I was freaking out because I had never seen palm trees before. I had never left the Midwest before. I could care less about whether or not I made it on the show, I got a free trip to L.A.! Tyra was a huge part of the show the first season. She was always there. We were going out to dinner and stuff with her. But I didn't care. I think that's why they liked me: because I didn't care. And about two weeks later we started filming.

I was excited to be on the show. I had never been to New York before. There were some stunning women, even though they photographed like shit, but that's what I learned: Just because you're pretty doesn't mean you photograph well. I just figured I'm gonna go there and not care, try my best and not really care if I win because I didn't really think I had a chance.

MR: What advice would you give someone who wanted to be on *America's Next Top Model*?

AC: Just be yourself, and if being yourself isn't interesting, make up a character. From what I've gathered it's worked for many girls who came after me. Everyone loves the bitch. Everyone loves the underdog. Everyone loves the diva. It's worth it now though because I hear they're at least giving out real prizes.

If you're not interesting, make yourself interesting. You could be the most beautiful woman ever, but that's not enough. I mean, do you see many interviews with Heidi Klum? No, because she's not very interesting. There's no way Heidi Klum would get cast on *America's Next Top Model*. That's why they haven't made a real supermodel on the show yet because they're not basing it just on talent, they base it more on character. I was the underdog nobody thought would ever win, that's why I got on the show.

My number one advice for anyone who wants to get on *America's Next Top Model* is not to trust Tyra. She's there to benefit herself, not you. You need to look out for number one.

Christopher Knight: That should be the number one advice for anyone auditioning for any reality show: They're not producing it with the perspective that it's about you. You're a cog in the wheel. It's about the show.

AC: Well, when I got on *America's Next Top Model* they told us the show was going to be all about us, but it turned out to be all about Tyra. When we did *Stuff* magazine, who was on the cover? Tyra. We thought she was just a judge; we didn't know it was going to be the Tyra show. So when I did the *Surreal Life* it was, in a way, like "I'll show you."

MR: Speaking of *The Surreal Life,* **can both of you tell me how you became involved with the show?**

AC: I was asked by my old agent if I was interested. At first I said no because I was already struggling considering my deal with *America's Next Top Model* didn't come through as planned. I didn't get the publicity that I needed to launch an actual modeling career. I was familiar with *Surreal Life* and I knew it was either a bunch of washed-up celebrities or porn stars, but then I was told that it could be like spring break—a paid spring break. So I was like, "okay!"

CK: I had been asked to do it before. I had been asked to do *Surreal Life 3* and I flatly turned it down. At the time I was working on a show on the Discovery Health channel with Eric Estrada, a work-out show. During the middle of the shoot Eric Estrada was asked to do *The Surreal Life* and he did it. So I was familiar with the show.

I had been offered other reality-type shows before like *Celebrity Boxing,* which I turned down. A friend of mine is partners with Corey Feldman's manager so I had been following what was happening with Corey. I knew that after Corey did *The Surreal Life* things began picking up for him a bit, but still I wasn't too inclined to do the show. But they asked me again this past year and I felt I was ready to get back into the entertainment industry so, as a step in that direction, I looked at it and tried to ascertain whether it was a good or bad move.

Everyone I talked to said it was a good idea, that the show had developed a cachet and its own industry following and that the show could only accentuate who you are. Now, if you're a person the audience isn't going to like then it's not going to be a good experience for you, but if the audience likes you it can be very beneficial. The worst thing that could come from being on the show would be that I find out I'm as boring as I think I am. So I decided to do it, and lo and behold, it was the right decision.

AC: (laughing) Twenty-minute answer! But you see, that says a lot about the two of us. Someone who doesn't give a fuck about what people think (pointing to herself) and (pointing to Chris) someone who cares about what everybody thinks.

CK: Yeah, she'll go far with THAT attitude. She'll start caring eventually. She just hasn't been out there long enough.

AC: I don't care and that's why I'm happy.

CK: She says that, but she really does care.

MR: How long was it from when *The Surreal Life* finished taping to when it began airing?

CK: Two weeks after it started. You only spend twelve days in the house. They have things planned for you to do and you're not sure what you're going to do next. You wake up in the morning and think you're going to have a nice quiet breakfast and then a bunch of kids come running into the house and you have to babysit them. On top of that you were up until two in the morning the night before.

AC: Speak for yourself. Four A.M. for me.

CK: The show is like a maze and they throw the mice in and then strategically throw the cheese in and watch everybody bump into each other.

AC: Yeah, the cheese is the two fully stocked bars and the two margarita machines.

CK: No, that's the polish on the floor so the mice can't even move. Anyway, it's an interesting social experiment.

MR: How do you feel about your experience on *The Surreal Life* now that it's over?

CK: I'd do it again. Frankly I think that all people should spend a week each year where they're taken out of their comfort zone and have to live with different people, learning tolerance, giving themselves a chance to see things differently.

AC: I think that if you had lived with twelve women for three and a half months like I did on *America's Next Top Model*, you wouldn't look back on the experience so fondly.

CK: Well, we weren't competing with each other on *The Surreal Life*. It's a totally different experience.

AC: They didn't show the best parts of us on *The Surreal Life*, like when everyone was nice to each other and had good things to say. Those are all the parts I hold dear to my heart and I wish they would have shown at least one or two of them.

MR: Chris, had you ever watched Adrianne's season of *America's Next Top Model*?
CK: No.

AC: He had no idea who I was. I never watched *The Brady Bunch* either, so whatever. I'm from the *Beavis and Butthead* generation. I could give a fuck about the morals of *The Brady Bunch*. No offense; it's a good show for people who aren't morbid and macabre like myself, but I don't dig that happy Barney crap.

MR: You guys are in the unique position of having fallen in love in the fishbowl environment that is reality TV. What was that like?
CK: It was totally accidental.

AC: I think it's great because whenever I want I can rewind and see our first kiss over and over and over again.

CK: You know, it is what it is. It was played out, from my end, reluctantly. Luckily for the two of us, on the show we were who we really are. If it weren't for the show I think most people would have a hard time understanding why we're together, but as soon as they watch the show they get it.

AC: I don't know, we're not that weird. You see young girls with older guys all the time. Women mature faster than men, henceforth it works.

CK: (laughing) Don't be defensive.

AC: No, I'm just saying. Just because you're a good actor and were able to go on *The Surreal Life* and make everyone think you are a great, wonderful, superb guy doesn't mean you're that way off camera. That's all I've got to say! (To Chris) You're naughty!

CK: We were from totally different ends of the spectrum, but maybe we're a perfect example of what happens in that social experiment: People who are totally different and would normally never find anything in common are able to come together because they're forced to live in the same house and get to know each other.

It's great because we have a huge audience rooting for us. Two people that get together and don't have anyone rooting for them are doomed. It doesn't matter how much they love each other. It's like Romeo and Juliet: You're doomed if you don't have people rooting for you.

Both Adrianne and Chris live in Manhattan Beach, CA, and continue to model and act, respectively.

STAT SHEET

PREMISE:
A musical reality series that conducts a nationwide search for America's next pop music idol

HOST:
Ryan Seacrest

JUDGES:
Paula Abdul, Simon Cowell, Randy Jackson

NETWORK:
FOX

YEARS RUNNING:
The first season debuted in 2002. The fourth season began airing in 2005.

CONTACT:
Web: *www.idolonfox.com*

PRODUCTION COMPANIES:
19TV (creator Simon Fuller's company) and Fremantle Media (which also produces *The Price Is Right and Family Feud*)

CREATOR:
Simon Fuller

EXECUTIVE PRODUCERS:
Simon Fuller, Nigel Lythgoe (19TV), Ken Warwick (Fremantle Media)

CONTESTANT AGE RANGE:
16–28

NUMBER OF APPLICANTS PER SEASON:
100,000

NUMBER OF CONTESTANTS CHOSEN:
Twelve per season (after audition episodes)

American Idol auditioners camping out in an auditorium (Photo courtesy of Jennifer Anderson)

AMERICAN IDOL

Hands down, *American Idol* is the toughest reality program in the history of television on which to land a spot. When it comes to viewer loyalty and fanaticism, no other show even comes close. Since one of the main goals of the show is to convince hordes of wannabe pop stars that *anyone* can be the next *American Idol*, a large percentage of *Idol* fans don't just watch the show; they audition for it as well. In fact, over one hundred thousand people showed up in person to audition for Season Four of *American Idol* in the six open-call cities chosen this year. And while I can't help you improve your singing or create your pop-idol image, I can tell you what to expect when you show up in line, and better prepare you for what the judges (and I'm not just talking about Simon, Paula, and Randy) want to see from you.

The *American Idol* audition process is a highly guarded secret—one the folks at the show *definitely* don't want you reading about, partially for the sake of the show's integrity and partially to keep other shows from copying it. But I've done my research, made some back-alley deals, and risked my neck in order to bring you all the information I could muster. And while I can't promise to get you into Round Two (like some ludicrous scam deals you can find on the Internet), I *can* give you the hard reality behind this behemoth of reality TV. Who wants to go to Hollywood?

The Audition Process

Once a year, the good people at *American Idol* hit the streets to conduct the largest television auditioning process ever conceived by man. While most shows are satisfied with holding their auditions in hotels or parking lots, *American Idol* flexes its auditioning muscle in stadiums and convention centers, filling thousands of bleachers not just with cheering fans, but with hopeful stars.

First things first: Visit *www.idolonfox.com*, the official Web site of *American Idol*, for up-to-date information on which cities the show will visit to hold open calls (it changes every year). The next season's audition cities are usually announced after the last episode of the previous *American Idol* season.

As of Season Four, to be eligible for *American Idol*, you must be between the ages of sixteen and twenty-eight and be free from any and all record contracts, music management contracts, or any other contracts regarding your image or life story. You must also be prepared to sing five full songs that show off your vocal talents. All songs will be sung a cappella (meaning without music). No rapping will be allowed; this is a singing-only show.

When you audition, bring two forms of identification (driver's license, passport, birth certificate, or Social Security card) and a release form, which you can print off the show's Web site (though you can also pick up a form at the auditions). If you're under the age of eighteen, you must be accompanied by a parent or legal guardian.

The clothes you wear to the audition must be free of all visible brand names, sports team names, trademarked characters, or celebrity likenesses.

There are no video applications for *American Idol*; all auditioning is done in person at an open call.

Got all that? Let's get into the fun stuff.

Open Calls

While most reality-TV auditions are full-day excursions, auditioning for *American Idol* is more like a weekend retreat. The average person will spend close to twenty-four hours in line before ever singing a single note in front of a producer or judge. Even if you happen to make it all the way to Simon, Paula, and Randy (which we'll get to a bit later), you most likely won't see them until the third day of your auditioning adventure. In fact, let's just dispel this myth right now: If you show up to audition for *American Idol*, you will *not* automatically get to sing in front of the "Big Three" judges. Over 90 percent of the people who show up to audition for *American Idol* never lay eyes on Simon, Paula, or Randy at all.

So if you're not making a fool of yourself in front of the "Big Three," what are you doing during all that time? The answer? Waiting. I've never heard so many tales of woe, endurance, and physical pain as I heard while interviewing *American Idol* auditioners. These people sit on the ground, packed like sardines, in the freezing cold, with sub-par bathroom facilities and overpriced food and water, for days at a time—just to get a chance to sing (if they still have a voice after all of that) for a judge who gives them less than thirty seconds to prove their idol-ness. No one said the path to superstardom was paved with gold!

Once you find out where and when the nearest audition is being held, it's time to make preparations. The call time at most auditions is 8 A.M. This means that 8 A.M. is the *earliest* the casting team will begin making announcements and/or auditioning candidates. But from what I gather, the auditions rarely start on time. And if you can't make it to the audition location by 8 A.M., don't bother showing up at all. In fact, if you don't make it there a few hours before 8 A.M., there's very little chance you'll even be auditioned by anyone. There are only a certain number of people the casting team can accommodate at a given audition location—so even if you're the next *American Idol*, no one's going to know it if you don't show up early.

Approximately 15,000 *American Idol* hopefuls filled Cleveland Browns Stadium and braved the drizzly weather during an open call audition in 2004 (Photo by Johanna Hoadley/Cleveland.com)

Most facilities don't allow people to line up before 6 A.M., but regardless of the rules, thousands of people still show up as early as midnight on the night before and simply wait in lines of their own creation until the official line opens at 6 A.M. Only for *American Idol* will people wait in line all night just to get into another line and wait all day.

Since you can expect to spend the majority of the night and day waiting in line to audition, the *American Idol* producers have created a list of appropriate items to bring with you. They have made these lists in accordance with the rules of each individual casting location, so some of the rules may change from town to town, but what follows is a list of the items you can bring to *every* location, as well as the items you aren't allowed to bring to *any* of the locations.

Items OK to bring

- Backpacks
- Blankets
- Foldable chairs (*must* be foldable)
- Pillows
- A small amount of food

Items not OK to bring

- Coolers
- Tents
- Alcohol or drugs of any kind

As for the auditions themselves, while not every audition city's process works in exactly the same way, for the most part they all follow the same basic structure.

Around 8 A.M. on Day One of the audition, an army of casting people descends on the patiently waiting crowd. Person by person, casting associates go through the crowd asking each person to sing a few bars of a song. "A few bars" usually means less than ten seconds of singing. Within those ten seconds, the casting person will decide whether or not you get a wristband, which will gain you access to the venue. While some people will get turned away for obvious reasons (too young, too old), and others will be sent home because they weren't good enough or *interesting* enough, from what I've heard, the majority of people get wristbands; I'm guesstimating somewhere between 80 and 90 percent.

As a side note, although you're allowed to bring as many friends and family members with you as you'd like while you wait in line *outside* the venue, you can bring only one person who is not auditioning with you *inside* the venue.

Everyone with a wristband is then moved into *another* line inside the facility. Most people will spend the majority of the day waiting in this line in order to audition in front of the producers and/or casting people. This phase of the audition process works similarly to the wristband phase, in that the producers and/or casting people patrol the lines asking each person to sing a section of a song (chosen by the auditioner). This time, you'll have about thirty seconds to sing, as opposed to ten. This is where most people are asked to leave—probably over 50 percent.

The lucky ones who are asked to stick around are moved to a different line, where they wait to enter a separate room to audition in front of the show's producers. Often this phase of the audition will be held the following day. Here you'll get a chance to do a "mock audition" in front of the producers, which will closely resemble the audition you may be asked to do in front of Simon, Paula, and Randy.

The producers will give you a chance to perform a big chunk of a song—enough to really show what you've got to offer. If they think you'd be an asset to the show (or an asset to the audition episodes of the show), you'll be asked to come back—ready for this?—*in two or three days*! In fact, many people who make it past this round actually sleep in the venue for up to three days, waiting for the final round of the audition (imagine the smell!). That's the bad news. The good news is, if you've made it this far, you'll actually get to audition for Simon, Paula, and Randy!

If you make it this far, you are also considered "on the show." That doesn't mean you're the next *American Idol*—it just means you have a chance at ending up in the show's audition episodes. You'll be asked to fill out a giant form asking you every possible question about your life. The casting team will then perform a quick background check to make sure you're not a convicted felon, make you fill out a bunch of legal forms signing away your life to the show, and ask you to wait for a few days until your name is called for the big audition.

Everyone who has ever watched the infamous *American Idol* audition episodes—the ones that kick off every new season of the show—knows how this phase of the audition process works. You'll walk into the audition room, say "hello" to Simon, Paula, and Randy, sing about thirty seconds of your song, and either get told you're the worst singer ever to walk the earth, or get handed a yellow ticket, accompanied by the magic words: "You're going to Hollywood!"

Three Easy-To-Follow Rules

While I can't help you win the show, I *can* give you some tips that will help you get some camera time and hopefully land a spot in front of Simon, Randy, and Paula. Once you're in front of the Big Three, whether or not you achieve superstardom is in their hands.

Rule #1: Know Your Role

There are two types of people the casting team looks for in the audition process: the best and the worst. You've got to know which category you fall into.

Contrary to popular opinion, the contestants who are going to be made fun of (i.e., the William Hungs of the world) are told before entering the audition room with Simon, Paula, and Randy that they don't actually have a shot at going to Hollywood, and that they're being filmed only for their "entertainment value." While the producers will swear up and down that this is not true, I'm telling you it is—because I've talked to many people who have gotten this speech.

These people know they're being ridiculed, and they don't care. They're told by the producers to act as though they really think they have a shot at going to Hollywood. William Hung became a cultural icon, made a little bit of money, and got to have a whole bunch of fun—all for making a fool of himself on national television. If you really think William Hung believed he had a shot at making it as the next *American Idol*, you're crazy. It's entertainment, people—come on! It's all in good fun.

WHAT THEY'RE LOOKING FOR

Kelly Clarkson, Ruben Studdard, Fantasia Barrino: These are the first three *American Idol* winners. If you stood them all in a line, you'd probably think, "What in the world do these three people have in common?" And that's just the point. If the show awarded the crown to the same type of person each year, it would be boring and predictable. What makes it exciting is the fact that you never know who's going to win.

The American voters can be very fickle, wanting to see the underdog win one year, catapulting the classic "girl next door" to stardom the next. It's anybody's game, and that's why the show has remained popular after all these years.

"We're looking for the whole package," Simon Cowell explains repeatedly. The judges want the image, the voice, and the personality. A good voice alone is simply not enough, and a pretty face on its own won't get you very far either. You've got to be what everyone else is not: You've got to be a superstar.

Know before you get in line what role you're going to play: the best or the worst. And if you don't think you fit into one of these categories, don't even bother showing up. The first people to go at every *American Idol* audition are the "middle-of-the-road" people. The producers have no use for mediocrity; an average person with an average voice does not make for good television. While mediocrity might get you a wristband and entrance into the venue, I can promise you that you'll be asked to leave after the next round. Seriously, I can promise you this: Only the best and the worst make it further than the wristband phase.

Rule #2: The Squeaky Wheel Gets Oiled

With thousands of people surrounding you in line, it's very easy for the casting people and producers to literally lose you in the crowd. You've got to stand out, make a big loud show of yourself, and do whatever you can to get attention.

If you fall into the "worst" category of applicants, a good way to make it to the "Big Three" is to wear an utterly ridiculous outfit. Half of the "worst" singers who make it onto the audition episodes get there because they look totally crazy. So wear your dad's old army jacket over a mental-patient smock, put on some snakeskin boots, and comb your hair over your face. As long as your voice is shockingly bad, you'll stand a good chance of making it on the show (the audition portion—not the actual singing competition, silly).

But whatever you do, *don't* look like a clown, and I mean this both literally and figuratively. For the casting team, the whole point of selecting the "worst" singers is to find people who *seem* totally serious. If you're a normal guy *pretending* to be wacky to get on television, it's not going to work; that works only on *The Gong Show*. The casting team looks for people who really think they're great singers with great looks, but who in reality look totally hideous and sing like polar bears. Basically, you need to look like a *real* crazy person—not a movie version of a crazy person.

And heck, if you show up looking crazy and singing badly and you actually think you've got a chance to win, then more power to you. But the producers will warn you ahead of time that you're going to be made fun of. If you don't break down and cry when you're hit with this revelation, you might just have a fun little moment of fame—and, who knows, you could end up being the next William Hung.

If you think you fall into the "best" category of singers, the same rules apply—just minus the looking-like-a-crazy-person part. It's important that the producers notice you and understand how badly you want to be the next American Idol. Do whatever it takes (while still retaining your dignity) to get noticed. You want to dress as if you were about to walk onstage for the biggest show of your life. Make sure your image (outfit, hair, makeup) matches your personality and makes you look like a star. Your look is at least 50 percent of what's going to grab the attention of the producers and score you an invite to the big audition. You need to have a big personality, lots of energy, and an obvious passion for becoming the next American Idol.

Rule #3: Spin a Good Yarn

Aside from a good image and good voice, the final element in the *American Idol* holy trinity of superstardom is a good backstory. The producers need to sell you to the American viewing public as a whole package. They want people to become invested in your story—to relate to your struggles and root for you to triumph over everyone else—and they're going to need more than your pretty face and voice to do it. Kelly Clarkson was the perfect American girl next door. Clay Aiken was the nerdy kid with the amazing voice that no one thought could make it to the top. Fantasia Barrino was the single mother with one last chance to make her dreams come true. Who are you? Your story has to be able to compete with these.

In fact, your story has to be *better* than the stories of the previous Idols, because the show will never cast people with stories exactly like those again. I often hear people say that Fantasia opened the door for other single mothers to make it on *American Idol*, and I just look at those people like they're nuts. You've got it totally backwards, people! Because of Fantasia, the casting team will *never* cast another person with a story just like hers (or at least not for a very long time). The show can't repeat stories, because repetition bores viewers. I hate to be so blunt, but it's television and those are the rules.

Know your story before you show up, and make it your mantra. If you're a country girl who's never been to the big city, then make that your story and stick to it as hard as you can. If you're the bad kid with a troubled past trying to turn his life around, then be that person to the letter. Tell your story to everyone within earshot while you're waiting in line. Repeat it to the producers so often that they could recite it back to you word for word. Become your character and let your life define who you are—and who you will be as the next American Idol.

The three rules set forth above are the best advice I can give to anyone who wants to appear on *American Idol*. If you don't have a great voice, an exciting image, and a powerful backstory, the best you can hope for is a quick moment of fame in the audition episodes. But if you really believe you have what it takes, then knowing what to expect and understanding the three rules should help put you in the best position possible at the next *American Idol* audition. Have fun, keep a stiff upper lip, and I wish you the best of luck. Hopefully I'll see you in Hollywood!

Did You Know?

Just how big is *American Idol*? Big enough to turn William Hung into a bona fide rock star. Just like all great rock stars, William tours all over the world, puts out Christmas albums, has dozens of Internet fan sites dedicated to him and even. . . dies of a heroin overdose? Well, that was the rumor floating across the Internet in summer 2004. In fact, the rumor gained so much momentum that Mr. Hung himself had to come out to the press to publicly prove himself alive and drug-free.

THE CUT

STAT SHEET

PREMISE:
Sixteen aspiring fashion designers live together in a Soho loft, testing their fashion, business, sales, and marketing skills to see who will become the next icon of the fashion industry.

HOST:
Tommy Hilfiger

NETWORK:
CBS

YEARS RUNNING:
Season 1 debuts mid-season 2005

CONTACT:
Web: *www.cbs.com*

PRODUCTION COMPANY:
Lions Gate Television in association with Pilgrim Films and Television

EXECUTIVE PRODUCERS:
Craig Piligian, Darren Maddern, Peter Connolly

CONTESTANT AGE RANGE:
18 and up

NUMBER OF APPLICANTS PER SEASON:
20,000

NUMBER OF CONTESTANTS CHOSEN:
Sixteen per season

Have you ever caught yourself saying "Oh, my god, I can't believe she's wearing that!" Do you walk through malls wishing you could hand out tickets for every fashion faux pas you see? Think an America dressed by you would look better? Well then, *The Cut* is your show.

The Cut takes sixteen fashion icon hopefuls, tosses them into a loft in Soho, and puts their fashion skills to the test. Each week a team of guest advisers, chosen by Mr. Hilfiger, chooses who makes the cut and who doesn't. The winner gets his or her own fashion line under Hilfiger's label, and that line will be sold in stores nationwide.

Don't get caught wearing white after Labor Day, and don't get caught auditioning for *The Cut* without reading this chapter! Away we go!

The Audition Process

As of this writing, *The Cut* has cast only its first season. The rules may change slightly in future seasons (for example, with the possible addition of video applications to the casting process), so be sure to check the CBS Web site (*www.cbs.com*) for the most up-to-the-minute casting information.

The show's first season was cast completely through open calls and street recruiting. Aside from casting associates visiting the nation's top fashion schools and handing out fliers to promote the open calls, they also stopped fashion-conscious people on the streets and asked them to come in for auditions.

The Cut isn't looking just for expertly trained fashion designers—in fact, to make it onto the show, you don't need to have any experience at all. As long as you believe you have a great eye for fashion, and as long as you can see yourself running and designing one of the world's biggest fashion lines, you'll be plenty prepared for *The Cut*. No sewing expertise needed!

Considering that the winner gets his or her own fashion line under Tommy Hilfiger's label, and will have his or her clothes sold in malls across the country, the show had no problem attracting wannabe fashion designers. In fact, more than five hundred people showed up at each open call.

The best way to ace an open-call audition is to be prepared. Here's what you can expect:

Open Calls

The Cut uses the group interview method at its open calls. After standing in line, filling out a short application form, and having your Polaroid taken, you'll be seated at a table with ten other potential cast members. The casting people will then pose a few questions to the table in the hopes of sparking some interesting conversation. I have to admit, I've heard lots of different group interview questions before, but *The Cut* has some of the most amusing ones. Expect questions such as: "Who's the worst-dressed person in this room?"; "Who's the worst fashion designer?"; and "Name one fashion mistake someone at this table has made." Sounds like the recipe for a catfight to me.

Your strategy at the open call should be to get heard. Make sure you leave an impression. Be the first to answer all the questions, and do your best to steer the conversation. You want to show the casting associates that you're a leader. If someone at your table hasn't said much, make sure to ask that person a direct question. When the casting people see that you're a born leader with a big personality, you'll be almost guaranteed at least one callback. The worst thing you can do is clam up—so even if someone else at your table is hogging all the talking time, make sure you get your voice heard.

WHAT THEY'RE LOOKING FOR

Most important, *The Cut* wants people who are fashion-savvy. You don't necessarily need to be formally trained in fashion design, but you have to demonstrate a deep passion for fashion and an understanding of why certain fashions work and others don't. One of *The Cut*'s casting directors said it best: "They have to know how to put an outfit together, but they don't necessarily have to know how it was made."

Big personalities are key. Also, what you wear to your open call and all subsequent interviews is really important. After all, if you don't know how to dress yourself and wow the casting department with your fashion sense, then how could you do the same for the rest of America?

If the casting team likes you in the group interview, then someone will ask you to stick around for a while and fill out a longer application. Expect lots of essay questions about all of your fashion opinions, as well as your educational, occupational, and romantic histories. Once you're done with the application, you can head home and wait for a phone call. It could take a few weeks, so be patient.

Round Two and Beyond

If the casting team likes you, they'll ask you to come to the nearest big city for a twenty- to thirty-minute taped interview. Be prepared to talk at length about every facet of your life. Make sure to let your big personality show. Let them know how badly you want to be on *The Cut* and what you, as a cast member, would bring to the show.

Then come the finals. The best of the best are sent to New York City to meet with Tommy Hilfiger himself, as well as with the show's producers and CBS network executives. After a series of interviews and medical and psychological tests, if Mr. Hilfiger thinks you have what it takes to be America's next fashion icon, you'll have made *The Cut*.

Did You Know?

Much like many of the contestants on *The Cut*, Tommy Hilfiger was a self-taught fashion maven. With no formal training, Mr. Hilfiger moved to New York City in the mid-1980s and quickly launched his first collection of menswear, including his revolutionary take on button-down shirts and chino pants. Within two years of moving to NYC, Tommy had made over eleven million dollars selling clothes to the chic and fabulous. Hopefully one of his contestants will be so lucky.

STAT SHEET

PREMISE:
An aspiring writer and director get the chance
of a lifetime: to make their own film with a
$1 million budget.

NETWORK:
Bravo

YEARS RUNNING:
The show aired for two seasons on HBO starting in
December 2001. Season Three began airing on Bravo
in March of 2005.

CONTACT:
Web: *www.projectgreenlight.com*

PRODUCTION COMPANY:
Miramax Television

CREATORS:
Ben Affleck, Matt Damon

EXECUTIVE PRODUCERS:
Harvey Weinstein, Ben Affleck, Matt Damon, Chris
Moore (Miramax Television), Sean Bailey (LivePlanet),
Dan Cutforth, and Jane Lipsitz (Magical Elves)

CONTESTANT AGE RANGE:
21 and up

NUMBER OF APPLICANTS PER SEASON:
20,000

NUMBER OF CONTESTANTS CHOSEN:
Each season centers on the making of a movie,
and each movie requires a screenplay and someone
to direct it. There can be as many as three people
on each writing and directing team.

PROJECT GREENLIGHT

Finally, a reality show that doesn't appeal *only* to out-of-work actors: *Project Greenlight* lets out-of-work writers and directors get in on the fun as well. Offering up-and-comers a shot at making their own studio-funded feature films has so far made for great television but only mediocre films. But is that a reason to be discouraged? No way. You gotta figure that Matt Damon and Ben Affleck, the creators, producers, and occasional mentors of the show, will eventually produce a hit movie from *Project Greenlight* and catapult a couple of industry outsiders directly into the spotlight. Why couldn't it be you?

The Audition Process

There are three roles you can shoot for in the *Project Greenlight* application process: reviewer, writer, and director. Let's look at each of them.

Reviewer

Don't think you've got the chops to write or direct a feature film, yet fancy yourself a movie critic? The folks at *Project Greenlight* would love nothing more than for you to sign up on their Web site during the next application cycle and help them wade through a few thousand scripts.

Reviewers are given the chance to read up to fifteen randomly selected screenplay submissions, then write a review for each script and assign it a score. These reviews and scores help determine whether the Hollywood hopefuls who penned the screenplays have a chance at making it to the next round. In addition to reading submitted scripts, *Project Greenlight* reviewers are also given the chance to review and score the top ten "Director Scenes" (i.e., submissions from directing candidates) as they are posted online toward the end of the application process.

Writer

Got the great American screenplay taking up space on your iBook? As long as you're not a "professional," meaning that you've never sold a screenplay to a studio or production company, been paid to write an episode of a television show, or produced and/or directed anything that either played on television or was released theatrically, then you're eligible to apply to project *Greenlight*.

Applying will cost you a nonrefundable $30, and will require you to read a few other people's submitted screenplays, review them, and assign them scores. If you're not interested in having your script scored by a bunch of strangers, or if you don't feel like reading someone else's opus, then *Project Greenlight* isn't the show for you. But think of it as good karma to read other people's scripts and give them honest reviews.

Now let's get to the rules for your script. Your screenplay must be written in English and be in the "industry-standard screenplay format" (if you don't know what that means, visit your local library and borrow a how-to book on screenwriting). It must be no shorter than eighty pages, but no longer than 140 pages. No adaptations of other works are allowed—no novels, short stories, films, comic books, or anything else. All scripts must contain the original ideas of the writer. Lastly, your script must be written with a $1 million budget in mind, so leave out the huge special effects, explosions, and big-name actors, because Harvey Weinstein, the producer, won't foot the bill for any of that.

Once your script is finished (and the show has begun casting), submit your screenplay as a PDF file to the *Project Greenlight* Web site, then sit back and wait for the reviews to start pouring in.

Director

Whether you're fresh out of film school with a short film under your belt or a seasoned camera veteran with miles of footage clogging up your garage, why not cut it all up into a three-minute masterpiece and send it to *Project Greenlight?* Those interested in applying to *Project Greenlight* as directors are instructed to submit a three-minute scene, directed by them and outputted onto a VHS tape. Unlike the requirements for screenplay submissions, directors are allowed to film any scene they like, whether it's an original scene or an adaptation. I would strongly advise all directors not to submit a montage of scenes or a "trailer"-style three-minute piece—instead, show the casting folks what you can do with a single three-minute piece of narrative.

As is the case with aspiring *Project Greenlight* writers, directors must have no "professional" experience as directors, writers, or producers, and will be required to pay a $30 entry fee for their video submissions.

Your video must also include written titles crediting everyone involved in the film, including directors, producers, and actors. In addition, if your scene is an adaptation, you must give appropriate credit to the original source.

Stay tuned to the *Project Greenlight* Web site for information on where to send your tape. Unlike the screenplays, directors' submissions get seen only by the casting team and the producers, so directors won't receive feedback online from their peers until the final ten scenes have been chosen.

Round Two and Beyond

The pool of screenplays is slowly whittled down, round by round, with the highest-rated screenplays advancing to a new round every few weeks. In the first round, the top one thousand scripts advance; in the second round, the top one hundred scripts advance. Each author whose screenplay makes it to the top one hundred is then asked to create a three-minute "screenwriter video," which gives the writer an opportunity to introduce him or herself to the show's producers and explain why he or she should be chosen for *Project Greenlight*.

The producers and the casting team then take over the process and select the final five screenplays, based on the quality of the scripts and the charisma of the writers. These five lucky writers are then flown to Los Angeles, where one script will be chosen to be turned into a feature film.

The process is a bit different for the directors. The producers and casting team select their favorite 250 tapes from the pool of video submissions. The 250 directors of those tapes are then asked to make three-minute "filmmaker videos," showing the producers who they are and what makes them worthy of being cast on the show. From there, the producers choose their ten favorite directors and assign each of them a scene to direct from one of the ten finalist *Project Greenlight* screenplays. Once filmed, these ten scenes are posted online for *Project Greenlight* reviewers to review and score. The three directors with the best reviews and scores will be sent to the finals in Los Angeles—and may win the chance to direct a studio feature with a $1 million budget. No one said it was easy to make it in Hollywood.

Did You Know?

Matt Damon, Ben Affleck, and Chris Moore teamed up in 2000 to create Live Planet Inc., the production company behind *Project Greenlight*. But Matt Damon and Ben Affleck got together and hit it big long before that when they won a screenplay Oscar for the 1998 film *Good Will Hunting*. Yet, that wasn't the first time the two of them had worked together. Matt and Ben officially graced the screen together for the first time in a T. J. Maxx commercial in the mid-1990s. I wonder why they didn't write a screenplay about that?

WHAT THEY'RE LOOKING FOR

It's a bit difficult to say what the *Project Greenlight* casting team is looking for, since every season of the show has been slightly different. But talent obviously plays a major part in the audition process. This is not to say that the best script or best director always wins, but unless your work is of a very high caliber, you don't stand a chance of making it out of Round Two.

Another thing to note: Yes, the folks at *Project Greenlight* are interested in making a quality film, and yes, they would love that film to gross tens of millions of dollars. But the real bread and butter for *Project Greenlight* is still the quality and popularity of its television show. If the people cast on the show aren't entertaining, and if there's no drama or emotion on-screen, then the whole show falls apart and it doesn't matter if the film sinks or swims in theaters.

Project Greenlight searches for average joes with little or no hope of making it in the entertainment world on their own and gives them an opportunity to prove their merits. If two struggling actors like Matt Damon and Ben Affleck can write a screenplay, win an Oscar, and become overnight superstars, it's only right that they try to return the favor to struggling writers and directors everywhere. Again, good karma.

My advice to the next batch of *Project Greenlight* applicants is to hone your craft, be yourself, and cross your fingers.

Acknowledgments

Over fifty casting directors and associates gave me the information I've passed on to you in this book. I extend to them my deepest gratitude for taking the time to answer my countless annoying questions, take my phone calls, reply to my E-mails, and bow to my backhanded threats (kidding).

Thank you to all of the cast members, producers, executive producers, and creators of reality television who took me into their homes, offices, and favorite saloons to lay on me the God's honest truth.

And lastly, thank you to the fans of reality TV who have stood in audition lines all over this great country, sent me eyewitness accounts of what they experienced, and helped me better understand what it is that makes so many of you pursue the reality TV dream.

To all these people, I say thank you for believing in this book. If it wasn't for you, the book would have been one paragraph long and would have gone something like this: "See here, my name's Matt Robinson. Yeah, I hear you're looking to land a spot on reality TV? Well, scram, kid. What are you looking at me for? Good luck, chumps!" (I have no idea why I would have become like Edward G. Robinson if the book had been so short. Maybe it's the last name. Anyway, let's just be thankful no one has to answer that question.)

A quick, specific "thank you" to the following wonderful, helpful people: Suzanne Budd, David Obst, Oliver Obst, Jena Pincott, Laura Neilson, Amy Ozols, Carter Carter, Lisa Gerber, Cara Dellaverson, Josh Assael, Justine Baddeley, Angie Hill, and Frank Reina.

Robinson, out.